CULTURAL ORIENTATIONS GUIDE

The Roadmap to Building Cultural Competence

THIRD EDITION

Joerg Schmitz

Princeton Training Press
a TMC Company
Princeton, New Jersey USA

Published by:
PRINCETON TRAINING PRESS
Princeton, New Jersey

a TMC Company
600 Alexander Road
Princeton, New Jersey 08540-6011 USA

Tel: 609-951-0525
Fax: 609-951-0395
Web: www.tmcorp.com
E-mail: info@tmcorp.com

Editor-in-Chief: Toby Frank
Cover Design/Illustrations: Sonia M. Rodriguez
Layout: Sonia M. Rodriguez & Colleen Fernandez

ISBN: 1-882390-28-8

Table of Contents

Foreword

The best managers and executives build high performance organizations. Research has shown these managers have the ability to identify the unique characteristics of individuals and help them apply their talents working with others. Now you have the opportunity to improve your executive skills in this area.

The Cultural Orientation Model is a tool. It's a lens that can help you see individual characteristics in a different manner. It can help you discern individual strengths and characteristics unencumbered by the common pitfalls of cultural stereotyping. This book is filled with information, skill-building exercises and material that will help you identify and use talent. You'll also learn about yourself. You'll learn how you can be more effective in negotiations, selling, and building productive business relationships.

Globalization offers us new business opportunities. It also brings new competition and challenges. The organizations and leaders who operate best across cultures will reap the fruits of success. We hope this work brings you success.

Nancy A. Curl

Multicultural/Diversity Leader, Management Development
IBM

Preface

The recipe for an organization's success in today's global marketplace is as vexingly complex as this marketplace itself: a global strategy, a matrix structure, a robust global brand, a reliable technology infrastructure, financial strength, market intelligence, and harmonized core processes are but discrete ingredients. Unleashing their power and establishing global competitive advantage significantly rests on how individual managers understand to apply the critical bonding agent of cultural competent leadership to the complexity and diversity of the global environment.

The cultural orientations approach, refined in over 17 years of practice in global management and leadership development, has become core to the development of cultural competence. This guide extends the approach outlined in Doing Business Internationally (2003) and together with the Cultural Orientations Indicator® has been applauded for its comprehensiveness, practicality and relevance. The use of this approach in both management development institutions and global companies attests to this. Among these are: Harvard, MIT, UCLA, Columbia, Linkage, INSEAD/CEDEP, the Center for Creative Leadership, as well as American Express, Avon, BASF, BP, DaimlerChrysler, Franklin Templeton, General Electric, IBM, Infosys, Johnson & Johnson, Mastercard, Merck, Novartis, Schering AG, Solvay Pharmaceuticals and many others.

The third edition of the Cultural Orientations Guide contains significant improvements. We have refined our treatment of the critical skills, namely cultural due diligence, style switching, cultural dialogue and cultural mentoring. In addition, sections 3 and 4 provide a concise process and guide for the development of these critical skills, thereby further enhancing the utility and practicality of this approach.

I would like to thank the many participants in my workshops who have brought tremendous value with their comments, questions, and contributions, as well as my friends and colleagues at TMC, particularly Danielle Walker, Tim Walker, and Rick Punzo. Sonia Rodriguez, Susan Scherer, Juliet Reiter, Esther Lewis and Toby Frank deserve my special thanks for their support and hard work on this guide. My deepest gratitude, however, goes to my wife Latha, and my daughter Christina, for their love, patience, challenge and encouragement.

Joerg Schmitz

August 29, 2002

Introduction

Culture is the new frontier of leadership in a world that is characterized by the fading of boundaries and borders and the increase of interconnectedness and interdependence of people, nations and organizations. Robert Rosen et al. boldly declares that "we stand on a precipice, stepping into a new era, a time of enormous change and uncertainty characterized by the emergence of the first truly borderless, interconnected global economy."

Cultural differences and similarities are an important facet of interactions between individuals in a world that is characterized by the constant movement of people across national borders, the globalization of business, and widespread social, economic and political change. A high degree of contact and exchange between cultures is redefining our world and posing continuous personal, social and business challenges. The increasing degree of multiculturalism challenges societies, organizations, teams and individuals alike.

While the competitive advantage of societies may very well rely on the openness, acceptance, and nurturing of its multicultural make-up, organizations need to welcome and leverage cultural differences; teams need to embrace the differences of constituents and create inclusive environments; individuals need to be accepting thereof and flexible in adjusting to practices that differ from those of their own culture in order to ensure their personal and professional success. In short, from the broad, social context to our most personal individual context, we are required to develop *cultural competence.*

This issue has received increasing attention in the recent literature on business and management. Peter Drucker, for example, recognizes culture as the "key competency for the 21st Century" and warns that "tomorrow's business challenges are less technical than they are cultural. Culture must be managed just like any other phenomenon." Following the same line of thought, John Viney, author of *Culture Wars,* declares that "Culture will be, as it always has been, of critical importance in deciding the relative fortunes of the major world economies. Those institutions and organizations that recognize and articulate this fact will have the lead on those that neglect it."

This guide is part of a broad array of tools and resources developed by (TMC) Training Management Corporation to assist managers and business leaders in the development of the cross-cultural awareness and behavioral skills that will lead to competency. It accompanies the Cultural Orientations Indicator®, web-based assessment tool yielding a personal cultural profile (see Appendix D for details on how to obtain your personal COI® and other materials).

Both tools are core components of a practical perspective on culture most appropriate for addressing the most salient learning challenges of individuals, including:

- preparing for international business missions

- adjusting to cultural differences as part of an expatriate assignment

- understanding and managing interactions in a multicultural environment

- framing and addressing the challenges of multicultural, global teams and partnerships

- building and maintaining an inclusive and effective organizational and/or team culture

- assessing and bridging the cultural obstacles in underpinnings of client relationships

This guide provides a conceptual framework and practical applications, to equip individuals to meet the challenges of multiculturalism accelerated by the forces of globalization.

How the Cultural Orientations Guide is Organized

The Cultural Orientations Guide is organized in four main sections supplemented by appendices.

Section 1. *Framing Cultural Competence* establishes the underlying assumptions of the cultural orientations approach and provides a framework for mapping cultures according to ten key dimensions. It defines culture, explains the Cultural Orientations Model™ (COM™) and Indicator® (COI®), explores the critical skills, and illustrates how all of these tools can help build cultural effectiveness in a business environment.

Section 2. *Exploring Your Cultural Profile* provides a key to understanding how an individual's particular cultural orientation affects experiences, perceptions, and interactions. Each orientation is defined, key identifiers are described, and learning challenges are indicated. In addition, this section identifies a structured process for converting the insights from your profile into improved personal effectiveness.

Section 3. *Building Cultural Skills* consists of information, tools, and exercises that enhance learning and assist in building and implementing the very skills that characterize cultural competence. It includes a worldwide survey of cultural orientations patterns, worksheets, scenarios, and tools for applying the cultural orientations approach.

Section 4. *Putting All Together* contains nine scenarios tha thelp you understand who to apply thye critical cultural skills. Each scenario is accompanied by specific questions to guide you in developing a constructive solution.

As a self-study guide, each section builds upon the previous one. You are therefore encouraged to work through the Guide sequentially. If you are already familiar with the Cultural Orientations Model™ (COM™), you will find this guide a thorough summary, a comprehensive review of key concepts, and a vehicle for continuing learning.

Section 1

Framing Cultural Competence

Successfully building cultural competence has at its foundation understanding culture and appreciating how profoundly our values, attitudes and behaviors are affected by it. The goal of this section is to explore and define the concept of culture, introduce its main components and dimensions, and develop an understanding of aspects of cultural competence as well as the necessary tools to achieve it.

Understanding Culture

Culture is a complex phenomenon and a difficult concept to understand and manage. This is reflected in the number of definitions researchers have offered to explain it. In 1952, Kroeber and Kluckhohn identified over 150 definitions, most of which described culture as a pattern of values, beliefs and behaviors that creates a sense of identity for a social group and its members. It encompasses such tangible elements as language, food, dress, religion, customs, and artifacts as well as intangible elements, some of which are a group's values, beliefs, and assumptions along with the emotions with which these are invested.

Many definitions capture the sense that culture is a complex, multidimensional concept that operates on both a conscious and an unconscious level in individuals and groups. Hofstede (1991) defines it as "the collective programming of the mind that distinguishes members of one human group from another." This perspective emphasizes the cognitive aspect of culture. Edward Hall, in contrast, defines culture as "a system for creating, sending, storing and processing information." He captures both the cognitive and communication aspects of culture. Defined simply as "learned behavior," as others suggest, highlights the behavioral aspects of culture.

The cultural orientations approach recognizes that in addition to the cognitive, communicative, and behavioral aspects of culture, a strong emotional component needs to be recognized. We have therefore defined culture as *the complex pattern of ideas, emotions, and observable manifestations (behaviors and/or symbols) that tend to be expected, reinforced, and rewarded by and within a particular group.*

Many approaches to culture focus on national boundaries to determine cultural boundaries. We view this equation of culture with nationality as too limiting and ultimately impractical. Culture, understood as an attribute of groups and as a social process, can be identified at five interdependent, yet distinguishable levels:

- **The societal/national level**. This level describes the dominant (i.e, expected reinforced, and rewarded) values, norms, behavior patterns, and practices that exist within a particular geopolitical and socio-economic environment.

- **The organizational level**. This level describes the pattern of dominant values, norms, behavior patterns and practices within an organization. This includes the business practices and processes that distinguish them from others.

Being able to describe organizational distinctiveness is key to ensuring that organizational performance goals are optimally supported by the members of its culture.

- **The functional level**. This level describes the dominant values, norms, behavior patterns, and practices that exist within a particular business/professional function. These are the patterns that characterize and distinguish, for example, marketing, human resources, research and development, and sales.

- **The team level**. This level describes the dominant values, norms, behavior patterns and practices that exist within a particular team. It recognizes that every group and every team generates a particular pattern of behaviors and values upon which its performance is based.

- **The individual, interpersonal level**. This level describes the primary level at which we experience culture, namely in our own values, behavior patterns, and emotional experiences in interaction with others.

At each level of culture, the role of the individual in cultural processes differs significantly: At the societal/national, organizational and functional levels the individual uniquely reflects and reproduces cultural patterns (unless he or she occupies a key leadership position). At the team and the interpersonal levels, the individual has more influence on cultural processes. Whether we want to understand cultural processes or change them, it is the individual, interpersonal level at which we need to start.

Consider the following:

In the United States, individual assertiveness is considered an asset and generally is expected, reinforced and rewarded. For most U.S. Americans, assertiveness is both linked to positive emotions and evaluated positively. It often inspires pride in oneself and admiration and trust in others. Behavioral identifiers of assertiveness in the U.S. include eye contact, a firm handshake, a strong and definite tone of voice, the absence of qualifiers (such as "maybe," "perhaps," "probably," etc.), and tentativeness from a speaker's words, as well as a higher frequency of control elements (for example, questions and declarative statements) in language.

Assertiveness is also linked to and expected in particular social situations. In the U.S., individual assertiveness is an important element in successful job interviews. The linkage of certain values and this particular behavior is specific to the cultural environment of the U.S.; it is not universal. Cultural misunderstandings can result when individuals approach interactions with different expectations and assumptions about values and their associated behavior patterns.

In job interviews, for example, assertiveness, valued in the U.S., often conflicts with values and behaviors that are expected, reinforced and rewarded in many European and Asian contexts. A European job applicant may greet the interviewer with a strong handshake and may make eye contact, but his or her frequent use of qualifiers, tentativeness, and a lower tone of voice may not communicate the level of confidence the U.S. interviewer requires for a favorable evaluation. An interviewer who is not aware that the threshold for evaluating assertiveness as overbearing, arrogant, and impolite is lower in many European contexts can overlook and dismiss valuable talent. An Asian job applicant's handshake may not apply sufficient pressure to create the impression of assertiveness as evaluated in the U.S., and he or she may deem it inappropriate to make eye contact or may use language that is relatively tentative. Furthermore, neither the European nor the Asian applicant may associate the context of a job interview with the expectation of demonstrating a high level of individual assertiveness.

> **Culture** the complex pattern of ideas, emotions,a and observable manifestations (behaviors and/or symbols) that tend to be expected, reinforced, and rewarded by and within a particular group.

The above example illustrates the profound effect culture has on critical business situations, indeed, critical aspects of our lives. It also shows the interrelatedness of the levels of culture. Although culture is an attribute of social groups, it manifests itself in the interaction between individuals. It is at the level of interactions that we can identify cultural attributes.

Consequently, we need to sharpen our awareness of how the values, behaviors and views of our counterparts reflect the cultural orientations prevalent in the social environments that have shaped them. And through interaction we will discover our own cultural values, behaviors and perspectives. The cornerstone of developing cultural competence is therefore an individual journey of learning, development and growth.

The Journey to Cultural Competence

Five discreet competencies can be isolated when looking at the learning process that leads to cultural competence.

These competencies are integral to a cumulative learning process that yields specific behavioral skills and practices.

COMPETENCY NAME	COMPETENCY DEFINITION
Open Attitude	Receptive to cross-cultural learning and maintains an open and productive attitude toward difference. Continuously challenges assumptions about other cultures.
Self-Awareness	Is aware of and knowledgeable about his or her own cultural preferences. Can articulate own cultural values, beliefs, attitudes, and how they are reflected in behavior. Can identify how differences between one's own culture and another's culture could lead to misunderstandings. Is aware of how interaction with another culture makes one uncomfortable. Can identify ways to adapt that will support cross-cultural interactions.
Other-Awareness	Recognizes the cultural values, attitudes, beliefs, and behaviors of others in order to develop new cross-cultural business skills. Correctly identifies the cultural preferences of one's counterparts and how these preferences are expressed in their behavior. Observes and articulates areas of shared cultural perspectives to find common ground. Gauges one's counterpart's willingness to learn about one's own cultural preferences. Identifies ways to build stronger cross-cultural relationships.
Cultural Knowledge	Has acquired, or can acquire as necessary, a comprehensive knowledge of other specific social and business cultures. Correctly identifies the general knowledge needed about a culture. Gathers specific business or industry knowledge to conduct business in this context. Studies how the cultures' outlook on life has been shaped by history. Can identify how in this culture conflict is resolved, decisions are made, problems are solved, people are motivated, performance is rewarded, relationships are established and maintained, negotiations are conducted, people are led. Knows where to get necessary information and builds networks of contacts who can offer insight into other cultures.
Cross-Cultural Skills	Has the necessary skills to work effectively across cultures in many different business contexts. Can translate cultural awareness and knowledge into skills. Improves his or her own ability to work in multicultural situations. Continues to refine and improve skills. Adapts own business practices or management skills appropriately to particular cultures and situations. Negotiations are conducted and people are led. Knows where to get necessary information and builds networks of contacts who can offer insight into other cultures.

Key Skills

We have identified four interrelated skills that define the critical skill set of culturally competent manages and leaders.

Cultural Due Diligence is *the practice of assessing and preparing for the possible impact of culture* and doing preparatory activities that involve (1) investigating and determining the cultural backgrounds and orientations of one's colleagues, counterparts, partners, clients, etc; (2) evaluating potential and actual gaps; and (3) developing a strategy for minimizing any resulting negative effects. It is a skill that is best exercised in preparation for management interactions and business engagements (partnership projects, etc.). In this process, you strive to understand the history, background, and experiences that have shaped the perspective, outlook, and value system of specific individuals and/or groups with whom you are communicating and interacting.

Style Switching is *the ability to use a broad and flexible behavioral repertoire in order to accomplish one's goals*. It may be the result of cultural due-diligence. Here is an example.

Jack Hanstead was appointed the head of a cross-functional global team in charge of packaging copy guidelines for the global organization. He was responsible for getting information from each of the regions and countries on their legal guidelines and requirements for copy.

His first task was to send two brief e-mails to his points of contact in each region stating the information he needed from them. Of the four regions for which he was responsible, only two contacts responded to his e-mails. Their e-mails provided nothing that met his request; rather, they provided information about themselves. After a few more days without any more information from his region contacts, Jack decided to write again to those people who sent him empty e-mails to provide a little background information about himself: his job role and title, why he was appointed to this team, what previous experience he had. The day after he sent this e-mail, both people wrote back. Not only was their e-email quite friendly, but they were both excited to be working with him and hoped to arrange a phone conference to speak in more detail about the information he was requesting.

Astounded by the responses, he decided to send a third e-mail to the other region contacts. In the e-mail, he included information about himself (his role, his enthusiasm to work with these people and his appreciation for their help), and he provided a systemic explanation of the purpose of the request and how their input would be useful.

Not only did they immediately write him back, but they followed up with a phone call. Within the following week, all of the region contacts had provided him with the information he needed or were in the process of compiling that information.

His ability to style-switch, to change from the short, impersonal and functional e-mail style to a detailed, enthusiastic and more personal e-mail style, resulted in receiving all the information needed and creating a network of people he could count on for future needs. In addition, he established trust, credibility and rapport at an e-mail level which could be enhanced with follow-up telephone calls and face-to-face meetings.

This example demonstrates how certain behaviors are easier to change than others. Although Jack was frustrated by the initial lack of response on the part of his counterparts, he was able to style-switch with relative ease in order to obtain the information needed.

Cultural Dialogue is *the ability to elicit cultural information through conversation, and thereby illuminate cultural underpinnings of behavior and performance, close cultural gaps and create cultural synergy.* According to Moran and Harris (1991), cultural synergy "builds upon similarities and fuses differences resulting in more effective human activities and systems. The very diversity of people can be utilized to enhance problem solving by combined action." This involves more than observation and active listening skills; it requires a better conversation along the principles outlined by William Isaacs in his important book *Dialogue and the Art of Thinking Together*. He sees dialogue as a powerful means "to reach new understanding and, in doing so, to form a totally new basis from which to think and act. In dialogue, one not only solves problems, one dissolves them. We do not merely try to reach agreement, we try to create a new context from which many agreements may come. And we seek to uncover a base of shared meaning that can greatly help coordinate and align our actions with value."

Cultural Mentoring is *the ability to facilitate cultural understanding and integration to a new and different cultural environment.* Whether it is assisting a new colleague in decoding the cultural norms of a new organization or team, helping two groups integrate practices, or coaching an international assignee in managing the difficulties of culture shock, this skill amounts to utilizing one's awareness and knowledge to bring about cultural integration and effectiveness in one's sphere of influence.

Your Cultural Competence Toolkit

The cultural orientations approach helps individuals to embark on the journey of building cultural competence and honing the key skills identified above. It is comprised of a series of tools.

- the Cultural Orientations Model™
- the Cultural Orientations Indicator®
- this guide and a comprehensive array of publications and Web-based performance support tools (see Appendix D for details).

In the following, each of these tools is briefly introduced an dan overview provided.

The Cultural Orientations Model™

This model organizes concepts identified by Kluckhohn and Strodtbeck, Hall, Hofstede, Hampden-Turner, Trompenaars, and Bennett into 10 cultural dimensions, 17 cultural continua and 36 orientations. It organizes the wide spectrum of variability in values and norms among human groups, cultural environments, and social situations, and provides a shared language for addressing challenges related to culture. It facilitates an open attitude and cultural knowledge, supporting the practices of cultural due-diligence, cultural dialogue and mentoring.

Quickview: Cultural Orientations Model

ENVIRONMENT

Social environments can be categorized according to whether they view and relate to people, objects and issues from the orientation of **control, harmony** or **constraint.** A **control** orientation is indicted by a strong attitude that the environment can and should be changed and molded to fit one's needs. **Harmony** is indicated by a need to build consensus and balance all interests. A **constraint** orientation is indicated by a need to act within clearly defined parameters set by external forces. A key question to ask is: How do the actions, behaviors, business practices and processes reflect either a control, harmony or constraint orientation?

TIME

Social environments differ in how time is perceived and used. A **single-focus** orientation is indicated by concentrating on one task at a time, while a **multi-focus** orientation is indicated by attending to multiple tasks and/or relationships simultaneously. Key questions: How are tasks/relationships handled? What are the implicit norms and values that guide behaviors?

A **fixed** orientation is indicated by primarily focusing on an exact measurement of time. A **fluid** orientation is indicated by having a secondary focus on the exact measurement of time. Key questions: How much attention is placed on the exact measurement of time? What is the implicitly acceptable variance from a stated time or deadline?

A **past** orientation is indicated by placing a high value on pre-established processes and procedures. A **present** orientation is indicated by placing a focus on short-term and quick results. A **future** orientation is indicated by placing a focus on long-term results. A key question: are decisions guided by a past, present, or future orientation?

ACTION

Social environments can be distinguished by the way they approach actions and interactions. An emphasis on relationship, reflection, and analysis indicates a **being** orientation. A focus on task and action indicates a **doing** orientation. Key questions: How is the relationship between reflection and action structured? Where is the emphasis? How much value is placed on building and maintaining a relationship as compared with accomplishing tasks and action items?

COMMUNICATION

Social environments can be distinguished by the value orientations that govern how individuals express themselves. An emphasis on implicit communication and reliance on nonverbal cues indicates a **high-context** orientation. A **low-context** orientation is indicated by a strong value on explicit communication. Key questions: How are meaning and information related? How readily do individuals assume hidden meanings in messages?

A **direct** orientation is indicated by a perceived value of conflict and a preference for its direct and explicit handling. An **indirect** orientation is associated with the use of implicit modes and/or third parties in conflict situations and tends to be associated with a value of conflict-avoidance. Key questions: What is the value of conflict, and what are the expectations for handling it?

Emphasizing and valuing displays of emotion and/or eloquent use of language in interactions indicate an **expressive** orientation. An **instrumental** orientation is indicated by valuing factual, detached and dispassionate interactions and communications styles. Key questions: How is the degree of instrumental or expressive behaviors linked to the notions of professionalism and professional behavior?

An emphasis on protocol, customs, and /or set processes indicates a **formal** orientation. An emphasis on dispensing with ceremony and protocol indicates an **informal** orientation. Key questions: What is the value placed on protocol, customs and set processes? How are they linked to behaviors and practices?

SPACE

Cultures can be categorized according to the distinctions they make between **public** and **private** spaces. This includes distance between individuals, the organization of work space, and how information is shared. It is often useful to think about cultural space in terms of two questions: How much space do people want around them personally or at work? How does this affect the sharing of information?

POWER

Social environments can be categorized by the way they structure power relationships. A **hierarchy** orientation is indicated by having a high degree of acceptability of differential power relationships and social stratification. An **equality** orientation is indicated by showing little tolerance for differential power relationships and minimization of social stratification. Key questions: How acceptable are hierarchical relationships? How does the value on equality or hierarchy guide behavior, business practices and processes?

INDIVIDUALISM

Social environments can be distinguished by the ways in which individuals define their identity. An emphasis on independence and a focus on the individual indicate an **individualistic** orientation. An emphasis on affiliation and subordination of individual interests to that of a group, company, or organization indicates a **collectivistic** orientation. Key questions: Do individuals identify themselves more through membership in a group or as individual contributors? What expectations does the group, company, or organization have of an individual's behavior?

A **universalistic** orientation is indicated by exhibiting a value of standards, processes, procedures, rules and laws to govern situations equally: A **particularistic** orientation is indicated by placing value on uniqueness, difference and situational context in determining the way in which issues are handled. A key question: What is the implicit understanding of and perceived need to comply with rules, laws, processes and procedures?

COMPETITIVENESS

Social environments can be categorized by how people are motivated. An emphasis on personal achievements, individual assertiveness, and success indicate a **competitive** orientation. Valuing quality of life, interdependence, and relationships indicates a **cooperative** orientation. A social group may be internally cooperative and externally competitive or vice-versa. Key questions: What values motivate individuals, the group or the organization? How do behaviors, decisions and processes reflect this value?

STRUCTURE

Social environments can be distinguished by their degree of tolerance of ambiguity and uncertainty. Environments that value adherence to rules, regulations, and procedure are considered **order** oriented and prefer predictability and minimization of risk. Environments that value improvization exhibit a **flexibility** orientation and tend to reward risk taking, tolerate ambiguity, and value innovation. Key questions: What is the prevailing attitude toward ambiguity and uncertainty? How are these attitudes expressed in behaviors, processes and practices?

THINKING

Social environments can be distinguished by the emphasis on and reinforcement of different approaches to thinking and conceptualizing. They can either expect, reinforce, and reward a **deductive** approach (an emphasis on theory, principles, concepts, and abstract logic) or an **inductive** approach (emphasis on data, experience and experimentation). They may also either emphasize a **linear** approach (analysis and segmentation of issues) or a **systemic** approach (synthesis, holism and the "big picture"). Key questions: How do people perceive the value of and relationship between (1) concepts and abstract thinking and (2) data and experience? How is that reflected in the way people argue and present information?

The Cultural Orientations Indicator® (COI®)

This is a validated tool assessing personal preferences toward and/or against particular cultural values and norms recognized in the Cultural Orientations Model. The COI identifies the direction and strength along the cultural continua identified in the COM. In other words, it classifies your orientation and assesses its relative strength.

> **Cultural Preference** is an overall favoring of a particular cultural orientation, perspective or approach.

To properly understand your results, it is important to bear in mind that it:

- is descriptive rather than prescriptive, displaying in an organized manner the preferences as inferred from your responses to the COI questionnaire;

- describes general *preferences for a given cultural orientation* not skills, abilities or particular behaviors;

- is largely restricted to work-related behaviors and situations;

- is subject to self-validation, as is any assessment instrument.

Your COI Profile Summary includes a diagram of the COM that displays all ten dimensions and shows your dominant preference in each of the corresponding scales. This profile enables self- and other-awareness, facilitating a gap analysis and the acquisition of style-switching skills and cultural dialogue.

This Guide and Additional Resources

The **TMC publication series** and **Web resources** are additional tools to support the honing of other-awareness and cultural knowledge, as well as the practice of cultural due-diligence.

This guide specifically supports the building of cultural competence by guiding you through the exploration, analysis, and utilization of your cultural profile in section 2, and by providing specific tools and applications in sections 3 and 4. These applications focus on:

Global Diversity Awareness and Inclusion Skills

In the international business arena and increasingly within global organizational structures, you will need to operate with an awareness of differences on a global scale and their impact on business and management. To motivate your workforce and optimize performance, you will also need to apply your cultural competence to create and facilitate an inclusive environment to help you transcend and leverage these differences.

Leadership Development

You may need to broaden your overall interpersonal skill base in order to be effective in a variety of cultural environments and/or multicultural situations. Your primary goal is to develop and understand behavioral adaptation for those orientations that differ from your own. It is essential that you establish a clear sense of the range of challenges you will confront in a multicultural context and are equipped with adaptive and effective communication strategies.

Global Business Assignments (incl. travel and relocation)

When you are preparing for a business assignment in a particular cultural environment, it is imperative that you clearly understand the pattern of orientations you will encounter in the given cultural context as well as the likely manifestations of that pattern in a business setting. You need to develop the skill to identify the cultural dimensions that are most likely to challenge your performance, and to utilize resources, tools, and exercises that can help you bridge the culture gaps between you and others.

Global Team Effectiveness and Inclusion

In multicultural and often in virtual teams, culture-based style differences can be the sources of (1) lowered effective performance and increased personal frustration or (2) the source of high performance. It is not only crucial to identify team members' cultural preferences, but also to use this understanding for the benefit of the team and all its members.

Section 2

Exploring Your Cultural Profile

By highlighting personal preferences within key cultural dimensions, the COI identifies a personal pattern of cultural orientations. This pattern reflects the multitude of social influences and personal experiences that uniquely define the individual. The individual interacts in a variety of social contexts on the basis of this pattern.

The inner circle in the figure below identifies some of the main social influences affecting our cultural profile. The outer circles identify the main cultural contexts within which we interact.

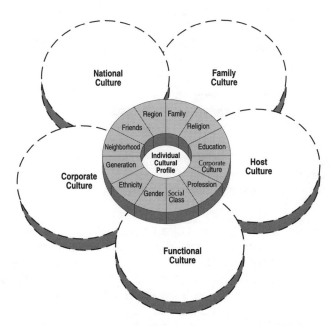

When reviewing your pattern of cultural preferences, you may want to explore which social influences have contributed to the development of those preferences and how you experience them in your relationships and interactions.

The COI profile helps us to explore an individual behavior, thoughts, or feelings in a given interaction, situation, or context and to highlight possible positive and negative consequences. The most significant value, however, is realized when using the profile to minimize potentially negative effects.

The stronger the preference, the more profound its impact on a given interaction and the greater the potential for a **culture gap** and the experience of **social distance** between individuals operating on different orientations or with a differing behavioral norm or expectation.

Culture gaps and **social distance** are experienced in interactions between individuals who have contrasting cultural orientations and/or in environments in which another orientation is expected, reinforced and rewarded. Cultural competence requires the ability to recognize potential or actual **culture gaps** in interactions, to adapt to and adopt strategies that will minimize these gaps. Since there is no direct or necessary correlation between a preference and a particular behavior, **culture gaps** or **social distances** can be experienced by an individual behaviorally, cognitively, and/or emotionally.

> A **culture gap** is the difference in orientation between individuals or between an individual and a social context.

> **Social distance** is the level of comfort or discomfort between individuals or groups as a result of differences in cultural orientations.

1. **Behavioral:** An individual behaves in a way that directly contrasts with the behaviors and/or expectations of the other. For example, a person with a fluid time orientation is consistently late for meetings with a colleague who is fixed-time oriented. The former understands appointment times as approximate, while the latter perceives them as exact. The experience of social distance caused by these differing preferences manifests itself behaviorally in this example. The behavioral manifestation of the **culture gap** may also be experienced cognitively and/or emotionally and may cause frustration and other negative feelings on both sides.

2. **Cognitive:** An individual is fully aware of a fundamental difference between expectations and actions. For example, a person who perceives time as fluid may report to a supervisor who expects fixed-time behavior. The fluid-time-oriented individual, cognizant of this gap, nevertheless engages in a variety of activities, such as setting a watch early or habitually arriving early for appointments to meet the other's expectations. The fluid-time-oriented individual experiences this **culture gap** cognitively; he or she is completely aware of the **social distance** created by two very different orientations to time.

3. **Emotional:** An individual experiences strong emotions, mostly negative, as a result of differing cultural orientations. These emotions can be mild, causing low levels of discomfort, uneasiness, or impatience, or they can be strong, resulting in overt or covert anger and aggression. For example, the fixed-time-oriented individual may get annoyed and frustrated and/or experience other strong emotions as a reaction to a fluid-time-oriented individual. The emotional reactions engendered by this **culture gap** may or may not be acted on or even conceptualized. In other words, the **social distance** may be experienced emotionally but not manifest itself behaviorally or even be in conscious awareness.

All three manifestations of a culture gap or social distance cause stress, tension, and conflict, externally and internally. This stress, tension and conflict need to be properly managed in order to increase individual effectiveness in a multicultural context. The three ways that one experiences cultural variation can be illustrated by the metaphor of the iceberg.

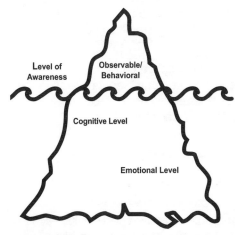

Level of Awareness

Observable/ Behavioral

Cognitive Level

Emotional Level

While behavioral difference is "on the surface" and therefore readily noticeable, emotional and cognitive differences lie beneath the surface and may remain largely out of awareness. The foundation upon which cross-cultural effectiveness rests is comprised of a sound understanding of the various cultural orientations, their impact on interactions and their identifying features.

Along with building this awareness is the challenge of recognizing how one's own cultural orientations affect one's perceptions of and feelings toward others. The COI Worksheet is designed to help you build this awareness and to guide you through the detailed analysis of each cultural orientation as outlined in Section 2 of this guide.

The COI helps you to identify those areas in which the difference between preferences is greatest, but it cannot predict the likelihood that they will manifest themselves behaviorally. A particular situation and how it is received by all parties significantly affects the individuals' and group's interaction.

For example, whether felt anger or frustration is behaviorally manifested will depend significantly on
(a) your relationship to the other person (whether you are the boss or the subordinate, the client or vendor, and so on.),
(b) what behaviors the organizational culture expects, reinforces and/or rewards, and
(c) the goal or desired outcome of the interaction.

Actively engaging with your COI profile and its dimensions, helps to
1. develop the ability to analyze the cultural content of situations and interactions, which requires some degree of awareness and cultural due-diligence
2. determine the optimal adaptive strategy, usually involving one or a combination of style-switching, cultural dialogue and mentoring
3. enhance the ability to style-switch and engage in cultural dialogue

The following pages are designed to help you interpret your personal COI. For each cultural orientation you will find:

- A **Functional Definition** that provides a general understanding of the particular orientation.

- A **Personalized Description** that lists general tendencies and preferences associated with individuals who lean toward that orientation. Special consideration is then given to possible consequences associated with strong or very strong cultural gaps.

Please note: We have given specific attention to possible negative consequences of strong or very strong cultural gaps. Seemingly negative statements serve to explain the possible *perception* or evaluation if your behavior expresses this preference and your counterparts expect the opposite orientation to guide your behavior.

- **Identifiers** or key patterns of behavior or ways of thinking that may identify a counterpart's orientation in a particular environment and/or interaction.

- **Primary Learning Objectives** that should be pursued to build a broader repertoire of cross-cultural adaptive skills.

The definitions, descriptions, identifiers, and learning objectives associated with each orientation are based on research conducted by TMC and our analysis of the basic concepts of the Cultural Orientations Model. For those orientations that are indicated as your preferences, you may identify with some of the descriptions and statements and reject others.

We suggest that you take time to reflect on them and determine which apply to you. This will enable you to focus your learning. We suggest that you mark those statements that apply to you. Guiding questions and space for notes are provided to encourage you to capture your thoughts on

- how you experience this orientation (in yourself and in others)

- the situations in which you tend to act on your preferences

- how you may have acquired a particular preference

- how learning objectives identified are relevant to you

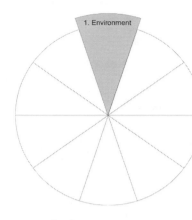

1. Environment

Dimension: Environment

How individuals view and relate to the people, objects, and issues in their sphere of influence.

Orientation: Control

Definition

Social environments that tend to expect, reward and reinforce a **control** orientation to the **environment** emphasize that people can and should influence and change their environment to fit their needs.

Description

You are a strong believer in the saying: "Where there's a will, there's a way," and you believe that your destiny is primarily in your own hands. When you encounter a problem, you immediately look for a solution. You approach the world with a natural sense of "empowerment." You view very few problems as insurmountable. You have a need for individual ownership of tasks and problems in your immediate environment.

You often assume that objects and people in your surroundings should conform to your preferred approach, methods and processes. You tend to be proactive, self-driven, and assertive and find that you naturally take initiative. You want to take charge of situations and do not shy away from conflict and risk. You get frustrated with people who do not seem to be actively engaged in problem-solving, do not share your sense of priorities, or who seem to lack initiative.

When this orientation is strong or very strong, you may:

- be perceived as aggressive and/or confrontational.

- assume that you will lead and direct in most situations.

- become easily annoyed, frustrated, and impatient with those who do not share your orientation and attitude toward problem-solving.

- tend to overestimate yourself and your ability to get things done.

Following are the identifying behaviors and values of a person with a **control** orientation to the **environment**. Check any boxes corresponding to a behavior you exhibit or a value you hold.

Identifiers

People with this orientation frequently:

- [ ] are among the first ones in a group of equals to assume a leadership role.
- [ ] display a high degree of optimism when confronting a problem.
- [ ] trust in, value, and emphasize pragmatic tools and techniques.
- [ ] advocate personal accountability and risk-taking.
- [ ] use declarative statements and closed (yes/no) questions with high frequency when speaking.
- [ ] display impatience with intangible and vague statements, assessments   and evaluations.

If you checked any of the identifying behaviors/values for this orientation, determine what your primary learning objectives are and rate the following in order of importance to you. Determine how you might incorporate these objectives into your behavior.

Primary Learning Objectives

Your learning challenges are to:

- [ ] approach new situations more carefully and slowly.
- [ ] develop patience.
- [ ] phase in your initiatives and contributions incrementally.

Reflection

1. How do you experience this orientation?

2. In which situations do you tend to act on this orientation?

3. Which influences and experiences have shaped your preference?

4. how are the learning objective relevant to you?

Orientation: Harmony

Definition

Social environments that tend to expect, reward and reinforce a **harmony** orientation to the **environment** emphasize the importance of balance with external forces in one's surroundings.

Description

It is important for you to maintain a balanced relationship with your social, natural and physical environment. You adjust your style and approach to the expectations and conditions of your surroundings in order to bring about harmony.

Decision making and consensus building with all parties in an interaction are key values that drive your behavior in social as well as business environments. Establishing and maintaining positive relationships is of key importance to you. You tend to avoid conflict and direct confrontation. You value flexibility and diplomacy and expect the same of others. When proposing a new idea or making plans, you readily accept that a compromise will be required. You dislike radical change and champion the careful contemplation and testing of innovative solutions.

When this orientation is strong or very strong, you may:

- be too conciliatory and appear weak to others.
- frequently avoid situations in which you are required to take a strong position.
- act as a facilitator when you are expected to provide clear direction.
- be afraid to make controversial decisions.
- shy away from assuming individual responsibility and accountability.

Following are the identifying behaviors and values of a person with a **harmony** orientation to the **environment**. Check any boxes corresponding to a behavior you exhibit or a value you hold.

Identifiers

People with this orientation may be identified by:

- ☐ a frequent use of qualifiers and open-ended questions when speaking.
- ☐ very gradual self-disclosure as relationships become more firmly established.
- ☐ a high degree of (visible) distress in confrontational situations.
- ☐ a frequently expressed need to assume the role of facilitator and mediator.

If you checked any of the identifying behaviors/values for this orientation, determine what your primary learning objectives are and rate the following in order of importance to you. Determine how you might incorporate these objectives into your behavior.

Primary Learning Objectives

Your learning challenges are to:

☐ articulate a position and opinion firmly without considering those of others.

☐ develop individual assertiveness skills.

☐ take risks when it would be advisable.

☐ decrease your resistance to change, at times.

Reflection

1. How do you experience this orientation?

2. In which situations do you tend to act on this orientation?

3. Which influences and experiences have shaped your preference?

4. How are the learning objectives relevant to you?

Orientation: Constraint

Definition

Social environments that tend to expect, reward and reinforce a **constraint** orientation to the **environment** emphasize the primary importance of external forces and conditions as defining parameters in human activities.

Description

You feel that you must live and act within the given limits of your environment. You see the world as immutable and trust that, in the larger scheme of things, situations will generally work out. You see it as presumptuous, even naïve, to claim direct control over organizational and/or business environments.

You often experience problems or resistance to your ideas or goals as obstacles that cannot be overcome. You generally accept the status quo and adjust your own behavior and expectations to the limits as presented to you. You do not feel naturally "empowered" to alter those limits in any way.

Your approach to problems and situations is often reactive and risk-averse. You prefer to behave according to a model and/or clear instructions and guidelines. You expect superiors or people in power to make decisions on your behalf.

When this orientation is strong or very strong, you may:

- be extraordinarily cautious when approaching an unfamiliar situation and/or task.
- require detailed instructions on a given project.
- need very clearly defined and delineated responsibilities and expectations.
- be perceived as obstructionist and inflexible by those who do not share your orientation.
- be insecure about taking charge in ambiguous and vaguely defined situations.

Following are the identifying behaviors and values of a person with a **constraint** orientation to the **environment**. Check any boxes corresponding to a behavior you exhibit or a value you hold.

Identifiers

People with this orientation may be identified by:

- ☐ their frequent references to and caution with respect to problems, obstacles and risks.
- ☐ their frequent requests for clear instructions and guidance.
- ☐ their use of passive and negative sentence structures.
- ☐ their references to pre-established procedures, processes and guidelines as binding and immutable.

Primary Learning Objectives

If you checked any of the identifying behaviors/values for this orientation, determine what your primary learning objectives are and rate the following in order of importance to you. Determine how you might incorporate these objectives into your behavior.

Your learning challenges are to:

☐   think of obstacles as opportunities and challenges.

☐   engage in creative problem solving and reduce the frequency of negative statements or concerns.

☐   take care not to hamper organizational dynamism and flexibility.

☐   be proactive rather than reactive when possible.

Reflection

1. How do you experience this orientation?

2. In which situations do you tend to act on this orientation?

3. Which influences and experiences have shaped your preference?

4. How are the learning objectives relevant to you?

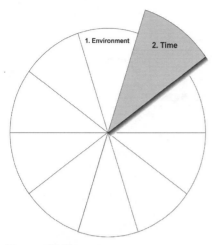

Dimension: Time

How individuals perceive the nature of time and its use.

Orientation: Single-Focus

Definition

Social environments that tend to expect, reward and reinforce a **single-focus** orientation to **time** and its use emphasize the importance of concentrating on one task at a time and demonstrate a precise commitment to schedules and timelines.

Description

You prefer to work on one thing at a time and break down work into a series of tasks, which you handle sequentially. You tend to have a high commitment to schedules, which you see as effective tools for ordering tasks. You are generally analytical in your approach to problem-solving. You consider it impolite or unprofessional to talk to several people simultaneously about different things.

When this orientation is strong or very strong, you may:

- feel overwhelmed when confronting complex situations, particularly when a quick response is required.
- believe that the quality of your work suffers when you cannot focus on one task exclusively.
- like to compartmentalize your work.
- organize tasks in discrete pieces to such a degree that you lose sense of the overall goals.
- rely on agendas, clear objectives, and guidelines to run effective meetings.

Following are the identifying behaviors and values of a person with a **single-focus** orientation to **time**. Check any boxes corresponding to a behavior you exhibit or a value you hold.

Identifiers

People with this orientation may:

- ☐ become irritated when they are required to focus on multiple things and inter actions at the same time.
- ☐ make an effort to sequence and structure tasks and work flow.
- ☐ compartmentalize and organize their work and personal space.
- ☐ display frustration when plans and projects have to be disrupted at the last minute.

Primary Learning Objectives

If you checked any of the identifying behaviors/values for this orientation, determine what your primary learning objectives are and rate the following in order of importance to you. Determine how you might incorporate these objectives into your behavior.

Your challenges may be to:

- ☐ feel comfortable when you must engage in many tasks at once.
- ☐ develop a tolerance for frustration when communicating with individuals having a multi-focus orientation.
- ☐ learn to reorganize and restructure on short notice with ease.
- ☐ remind yourself often of the long-term goals of a given project.

Reflection

1. How do you experience this orientation?

2. In which situations do you tend to act on this orientation?

3. Which influences and experiences have shaped your preference?

4. How are the learning objectives relevant to you?

Orientation: Multi-Focus

Definition

Social environments that tend to expect, reward and reinforce a **multi-focus** orientation to **time** and its use emphasize the importance of paying attention to multiple tasks and relationships simultaneously.

Description

You prefer to work on a variety of tasks and/or relationships at the same time. You are not likely to be disturbed by unpredictable and unscheduled events. You seek dynamism in your environment and welcome change. You tend to be easily bored when you are asked to concentrate on one issue exclusively.

When this orientation is strong or very strong, you may:

- be perceived as scattered by those who do not share your orientation.

- appear disrespectful to those who expect you to extend your full attention to them.

- be bored and/or frustrated with people who focus exclusively on one issue at a time.

Following are the identifying behaviors and values of a person with a **multi-focus** orientation to **time**. Check any boxes corresponding to a behavior you exhibit or a value you hold.

Identifiers

People with this orientation may:

- ☐ frequently engage in multiple activities at the same time, e.g., write letters while conducting a telephone conversation.
- ☐ bring up issues that are not related to the main topic.
- ☐ become visibly irritated when forced to pay exclusive attention to one person, issue, or question for an extended period of time.
- ☐ express feelings of boredom when having to devote themselves to one thing for an extended period of time.

Primary Learning Objectives

If you checked any of the identifying behaviors/values for this orientation, determine what your primary learning objectives are and rate the following in order of importance to you. Determine how you might incorporate these objectives into your behavior.

You may find it challenging to:

- ☐ develop a tolerance for frustration when dealing with individuals of a single-focus orientation.
- ☐ address discrete issues sequentially.
- ☐ see projects through to completion.
- ☐ respect the work processes of single-focused people whom you manage or to whom you report.
- ☐ limit the number of changes you introduce into your work environment.

Reflection

1. How do you experience this orientation?

2. In which situations do you tend to act on this orientation?

3. Which influences and experiences have shaped your preference?

4. How are the learning objectives relevant to you?

Orientation: Fixed

Definition

Social environments that tend to expect, reward and reinforce a **fixed** orientation to **time** and its use emphasize the importance of defining and managing time precisely.

Description

For you, events are critically determined and affected by time. Time is highly valued and needs to be controlled and managed. You think of time in precisely defined and discrete chunks. Punctuality is important to you. Good time management defines much of your behavior. You tend to view this as a critical professional attribute. To your way of thinking, planning and preparation are intricately connected to time. You take schedules, deadlines and commitments very seriously.

When this orientation is strong or very strong, you may:

- be perceived as rigid and inflexible by those who do not share your orientation.
- be perceived as lacking commitment to the overall goals due to your rejection of responsibilities and tasks that would change your plans and prior commitments.
- spend time trying to plan and structure events that do not lend themselves to such precision.
- easily get (visibly) frustrated and irritated with people who value time differently.
- often seem rushed to others.
- focus on the strict adherence to prearranged schedules but not give due consideration to overall purpose and context.

Following are the identifying behaviors and values of a person with a **fixed** orientation to **time**. Check any boxes corresponding to a behavior you exhibit or a value you hold.

Identifiers

People with this orientation may be identified by:

- ☐ their frequent mention of and reference to time and time constraints.
- ☐ a propensity for planning and scheduling.
- ☐ the need to structure events precisely.
- ☐ their irritability when plans and priorities take longer than expected.

Primary Learning Objectives

If you checked any of the identifying behaviors/values for this orientation, determine what your primary learning objectives are and rate the following in order of importance to you. Determine how you might incorporate these objectives into your behavior.

You may find it challenging to:

- ☐ see time as relative rather than as absolute.
- ☐ develop patience for business situations that are determined by a fluid time orientation.
- ☐ build in flexibility when scheduling and establishing timelines.

Reflection

1. How do you experience this orientation?

2. In which situations do you tend to act on this orientation?

3. Which influences and experiences have shaped your preference?

4. How are the learning objectives relevant to you?

Orientation: Fluid

Definition

Social environments that expect, reward and reinforce a **fluid** orientation to **time** and its use emphasize time as a loosely defined and relatively abundant resource.

Description

You recognize time as an important framework for life's events, but do not feel the need to control and manage it precisely. You do not believe that time can or should be tightly defined and tracked. You tend to see timelines and deadlines as expressions of intent but do not feel bound by them during work processes and events.

You focus on what happens within time, and you let situations and events rather than schedules determine your course of action. You focus on the people with whom you are interacting and/or the tasks with which you are involved and feel that it is imperative to meet their needs before being able to focus on other issues. You have an open-ended approach to planning.

When this orientation is strong or very strong, you may:

- lose sight of time as a key requirement for organizational effectiveness and profitability.
- often be asked to justify your focus on relationships by those who do not share your orientation.
- be seen as unprofessional by those who consider punctuality critical to professionalism.
- frustrate those who rely on you to get work accomplished according to tight schedules and timelines.

Following are the identifying behaviors and values of a person with a **fluid** orientation to **time**. Check any boxes corresponding to a behavior you exhibit or a value you hold.

Identifiers

People with this orientation frequently:

- ☐ emphasize the requirements of situations and relationships in determining business processes.
- ☐ treat schedules and timelines as approximate.
- ☐ show up late to meetings and turn in work later than expected.
- ☐ lack understanding for the frustration experienced by more fixed-time-oriented individuals.
- ☐ express a preference for spontaneity and a resistance to long-term planning.

Primary Learning Objectives

If you checked any of the identifying behaviors/values for this orientation, determine what your primary learning objectives are and rate the following in order of importance to you. Determine how you might incorporate these objectives into your behavior.

You may need to:

- ☐ turn in work on time or establish new schedules when necessary.
- ☐ respect fixed-time-oriented organizational processes.
- ☐ identify the operative sense of time in a given environment or situation and adjust accordingly.
- ☐ develop behavioral routines that enable meeting precise deadlines and timelines.

Reflection

1. How do you experience this orientation?

2. In which situations do you tend to act on this orientation?

3. Which influences and experiences have shaped your preference?

4. How are the learning objectives relevant to you?

Orientation: Past

Definition

Social environments that tend to expect, reward and reinforce a **past** orientation to **time** and its use emphasize the importance of stability and continuity with traditions.

Description

You look to the past as a guide and model for your present and future behavior. You tend to judge plans and changes according to whether or not they adhere to tradition. Continuity with the past is of great concern to you, and your behavior is guided by the need to preserve consistency. You have an intuitive sense of the importance of history and value the achievements of previous generations. You may experience change as threatening. You are not easily intrigued by novelties and require a relatively long period of time to assess and evaluate situations and opportunities. Precedents and past successes are important in solving problems and making decisions.

When this orientation is strong or very strong, you may:

- ☐ be perceived as blocking or resisting initiatives to improve work processes.
- ☐ feel irritated and threatened by rapid and frequent change.
- ☐ overlook or disregard potential for critical innovation.
- ☐ be perceived as not taking action quickly enough.
- ☐ resist change although it is not in your control to do so.

Following are the identifying behaviors and values of a person with a **past** orientation to **time**. Check any boxes corresponding to a behavior you exhibit or a value you hold.

Identifiers

People with this orientation frequently:

- ☐ exude a sense of stability.
- ☐ allude to past models and traditions.
- ☐ voice concern over a lack of stability and continuity with the past.
- ☐ display skepticism in the face of novel ideas, concepts and proposed changes.

If you checked any of the identifying behaviors/values for this orientation, determine what your primary learning objectives are and rate the following in order of importance to you. Determine how you might incorporate these objectives into your behavior.

Primary Learning Objectives

You may need to:

- ☐ practice visioning, long-term planning and projecting that diverge from the past.
- ☐ focus on present requirements and strategies to optimize the outcome over the short-term.
- ☐ listen more carefully to potential advantages of something new before discounting it.
- ☐ resist blocking initiatives that require a change in proven processes.

Reflection

1. How do you experience this orientation?

2. In which situations do you tend to act on this orientation?

3. Which influences and experiences have shaped your preferences?

4. How are the learning objectives relevant to you?

Orientation: Present

Definition

Social environments that tend to expect, reward and reinforce a **present** orientation to **time** and its use emphasize the importance of quick, short-term results.

Description

You are guided by concerns over the present and short-term future. You are motivated by promises of quick results and returns. You prefer handling immediate day-to-day problems or crises. Your planning is based on the demands of the moment, and you tend to have a keen sense of requirements as they affect your business today. You are a skilled crisis manager and a good tactician.

When this orientation is strong or very strong, you may:

- neglect the broad developmental view needed for essential strategic thinking.

- overemphasize the needs of the moment and neglect the long-range perspective.

- not fully appreciate the importance of history in business relationships and processes.

- be highly skeptical of long-range plans.

Following are the identifying behaviors and values of a person with a **present** orientation to **time**. Check any boxes corresponding to a behavior you exhibit or a value you hold.

Identifiers

People with this orientation may frequently:

- ☐ emphasize present opportunities.
- ☐ seem rushed.
- ☐ emphasize immediate results short-term profits and pay-offs to the exclusion of long-term benefits.
- ☐ seem irritated with or critical of requests for long-term plans and projections.

Primary Learning Objectives

If you checked any of the identifying behaviors/values for this orientation, determine what your primary learning objectives are and rate the following in order of importance to you. Determine how you might incorporate these objectives into your behavior.

Some of your challenges will be to:

- ☐ recognize the significance and importance of history, tradition and consistency for past-oriented individuals.
- ☐ understand how the past has shaped the present and how it may be valuable for planning the future.
- ☐ practice long-term organizational planning with an eye to the past and future.

Reflection

1. How do you experience this orientation?

2. In which situations do you tend to act on this orientation?

3. Which influences and experiences have shaped your preference?

4. How are the learning objectives relevant to you?

Orientation: Future

Definition

Social environments that tend to expect, reward and reinforce a **future** orientation to **time** and its use emphasize the importance of trading short-term gains for long-term results and benefits.

Description

You are guided by concerns over the long-term future. You tend to base planning and problem-solving on long-term projections. You evaluate the present by its potential for the future and judge ideas based on their benefits for the long term.

You have little problem envisioning a future that is radically different from both the past and the present. Indeed, your actions in the present are often motivated by the desire to attain this different future. You welcome and frequently champion change, but only if you are confident that it will be profitable and beneficial in the long run.

When this orientation is strong or very strong, you may:

- be so visionary that you neglect the requirements of the moment.

- underestimate problems, crises and opportunities in the present.

- lock yourself and perhaps your organization into long-term commitments that may significantly reduce flexibility.

Following are the identifying behaviors and values of a person with a **future** orientation to **time**. Check any boxes corresponding to a behavior you exhibit or a value you hold.

Identifiers

People with this orientation frequently:

- ☐ voice concerns about the long-term impact of decisions.
- ☐ are preoccupied with the future and articulate a long-range vision.
- ☐ exhibit high tolerance for frustration and are not taken off course by setbacks.

Primary Learning Objectives

If you checked any of the identifying behaviors/values for this orientation, determine what your primary learning objectives are and rate the following in order of importance to you. Determine how you might incorporate these objectives into your behavior.

You may find it a challenge to:

☐ focus on present requirements and strategies to optimize the outcome over the short-term

☐ recognize the significance and importance of history, tradition and consistency for past-oriented individuals.

☐ take into account immediate concerns when you are considering a plan of action.

Reflection

1. How do you experience this orientation?

2. In which situations do you tend to act on this orientation?

3. Which influences and experiences have shaped your preference?

4. How are the learning objectives relevant to you?

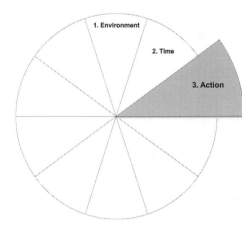

1. Environment

2. Time

3. Action

Dimension: Action

How individuals conceptualize actions and interactions with people and objects in their environment.

Orientation: Being

Definition

Social environments that tend to expect, reward and reinforce a **being** orientation to **action** and interaction stress the importance of relationships, contemplation, reflection and analysis.

Description

In interactions, you are guided by a concern for building and maintaining good relationships with those around you. You are motivated by good, trusting interpersonal relations and expect that building such relationships is a function of time, experience with each other, and incremental self-disclosure. For you, relationship building often takes precedence over accomplishing tasks quickly.

You may have a need to surround yourself with a permanent group of trusted individuals. When meeting new people in business, you require a relatively long "warm-up" period. You are careful not to extend trust too quickly. It is important for you that individuals establish their credibility and reliability. Before taking action, you need time to contemplate and reflect.

You tend to scrutinize issues carefully. You do not jump to conclusions or take action quickly or lightly and you feel it is important that decisions are well-founded and well-grounded.

When this orientation is strong or very strong, you may:

- need a very long time before being able to extend trust.
- hamper your effectiveness on short-term team projects through the long warm-up period you require.
- be rather inaccessible due to a permanent group of trusted individuals that surrounds you.
- be susceptible to "groupthink."
- suffer from "analysis-paralysis."
- impede flexibility and responsiveness due to your relatively slow decision-making processes.

Following are the identifying behaviors and values of a person with a **being** orientation to **action**. Check any boxes corresponding to a behavior you exhibit or a value you hold.

Identifiers

People with this orientation frequently:

- ☐ invest considerable time and effort in building relationships.
- ☐ are skeptical of unfamiliar people.
- ☐ approach new social and/or business situations cautiously.
- ☐ prepare for their activities well and do not jump into action.
- ☐ require a lot of information and consultation before making a decision.

Primary Learning Objectives

If you checked any of the identifying behaviors/values for this orientation, determine what your primary learning objectives are and rate the following in order of importance to you. Determine how you might incorporate these objectives into your behavior.

Your challenges may be to:

- ☐ develop a comfort level with making decisions and determining actions based on limited and/or incomplete information.
- ☐ focus on tasks and de-emphasize relationship building.
- ☐ engage in business relationships with people whom you do not know well when it is advantageous for your organization.
- ☐ be accessible to people outside of your circle of trusted confidantes and business associates.

Reflection

1. How do you experience this orientation?

2. In which situations do you tend to act on this orientation?

3. Which influences and experiences have shaped your preference?

4. How are the learning objectives relevant to you?

Orientation: Doing

Definition

Social environments that tend to expect, reward and reinforce a **doing** orientation to **action** and interaction stress the importance of task- and achievement-oriented behaviors.

Description

In interactions, you focus on accomplishing tasks quickly and tend to emphasize measurable achievements. You are pragmatic in your approach to completing tasks, making decisions and building relationships. You view business relationships as functional; they exist to get a task done. Once your counterparts have signaled their interest in doing business with you, you extend trust readily in order to focus on the speedy accomplishment of tasks. You may not expect relationships to last beyond the particular task to be accomplished.

When contemplating actions and activities, you are guided by considerations of the quickest and shortest path to accomplishing particular tasks and achieving preconceived goals. You often feel that any action is better than inaction. You are generally comfortable with making a decision or mapping a course of action even when detailed information is not available. You locate required resources easily and tend to be a pragmatic, quick and effective problem solver.

When this orientation is strong or very strong, you may:

- emphasize quantity of output over quality.
- approach relationships too pragmatically and be perceived as abrupt, cold, uncaring, or lacking in sensitivity and tact.
- overlook the importance and intricacies of building and maintaining relationships.
- easily dismiss the necessity of acknowledging and rewarding loyalty.
- neglect important details that may prove critical to accomplishing a task.

Following are the identifying behaviors and values of a person with a **doing** orientation to **action**. Check any boxes corresponding to a behavior you exhibit or a value you hold.

Identifiers

People with this orientation frequently:

- ☐ focus exclusively on "getting the job done" rather than on furthering a relationship with the people who are accomplishing a given task.
- ☐ end relations with others once the task that led to the relationship is accomplished.
- ☐ make decisions swiftly and focus on the speedy implementation of a plan.
- ☐ get impatient when asked to contemplate and consider issues at length and in detail.

Primary Learning Objectives

If you checked any of the identifying behaviors/values for this orientation, determine what your primary learning objectives are and rate the following in order of importance to you. Determine how you might incorporate these objectives into your behavior.

You may need to:

- ☐ spend more time gathering detailed and complete information before making a decision or setting the direction.
- ☐ focus on interpersonal relationship building and maintenance when doing business with being-oriented people.
- ☐ concentrate less on output and pragmatism in order to meet the needs of others.
- ☐ try to understand the significance to your business counterparts of long-term relationship building.

Reflection

1. How do you experience this orientation?

2. In which situations do you tend to act on this orientation?

3. Which influences and experiences have shaped your preference?

4. How are the learning objectives relevant to you?

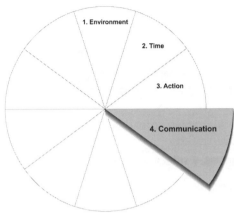

Dimension: Communication

How individuals express themselves.

Orientation: High Context

Definition

Social environments that tend to expect, reward and reinforce a **high-context** orientation to **communication** emphasize the value of implicit communication.

Description

As a high-context communicator, you hold symbolism and propriety in high esteem and value behavior more than words. You are very sensitive to a wide array of situational components and tend to extract meaning from a vast variety of sources. You rely on nonverbal, symbolic and situational cues more than on verbal and written cues. You value the indirect and artful use of language and tend to imply rather than state what you mean. In order to get work done, you require a lot of contextual information about those with whom you are communicating and/or conducting business.

When this orientation is strong or very strong, you may:

- cause significant misunderstanding because of your heavy reliance on symbolic language and indirect methods of communicating.

- cause confusion among colleagues and counterparts who do not share your orientation and who find your intentions and expectations ambiguous.

- mistakenly assume that the individuals with whom you work share and understand your frame of reference, which is particularly problematic in a multi cultural workplace.

- create a high degree of frustration in lower-context individuals, who may see you as distrustful or lacking confidence in them.

Following are the identifying behaviors and values of a person with a **high-context** orientation to **communication**. Check any boxes corresponding to a behavior you exhibit or a value you hold.

Identifiers

Individuals with this orientation frequently:

- ☐ distinguish themselves by excellent observational and listening skills.
- ☐ have well-developed interactional acuity and astuteness.
- ☐ are concerned with how others may interpret situations and often ask for others' interpretations of the same situation.
- ☐ communicate in a detail-oriented manner and attach great significance to non verbal elements of communication.
- ☐ are conscientious and sensitive to the summary effect of all aspects of situations and interactions.

Primary Learning Objectives

If you checked any of the identifying behaviors/values for this orientation, determine what your primary learning objectives are and rate the following in order of importance to you. Determine how you might incorporate these objectives into your behavior.

Your learning challenges may include:

- ☐ not interpreting low-context individuals as impolite or less savvy.
- ☐ identifying the ambiguous ways you communicate with others.
- ☐ ensuring comprehension and a shared frame of reference with your business associates.
- ☐ correcting miscommunication diligently.
- ☐ communicating expectations explicitly.
- ☐ focusing on explicit meaning.

Reflection

1. How do you experience this orientation?

2. In which situations do you tend to act on this orientation?

3. Which influences and experiences have shaped your preference?

4. How are the learning objectives relevant to you?

Orientation: Low Context

Definition

Social environments that tend to expect, reward and reinforce a **low-context** orientation to **communication** emphasize the value of explicit communication.

Description

As a low-context communicator, you value words and documentation. You explicitly state what you mean and tend to view and use language pragmatically and with precision. For you, successful communication is directly tied to the literal meaning of the words used. You tend to value the processes of choosing and interpreting words. Written messages and detailed documentation have more value and significance to you than information conveyed orally or personally. You need little contextual information about those with whom you communicate and/or conduct business. You place great value on good and precise oral and written communication skills and the maintenance of records.

When this orientation is strong or very strong, you may;

- find that your level of explicitness and reliance on written communication may alienate higher-context communicators with whom you interact.
- discover that higher-context counterparts may feel patronized or insulted by what may be perceived as "stating the obvious."
- be perceived as cold and indifferent.
- miss important information conveyed in a non- or extra-verbal manner.

Following are the identifying behaviors and values of a person with a **low-context** orientation to **communication**. Check any boxes corresponding to a behavior you exhibit or a value you hold.

Identifiers

Individuals with this orientation frequently:

- ☐ require that meaningful and significant information be recorded meticulously.
- ☐ are good record keepers.
- ☐ are prolific writers.
- ☐ ask for and provide explicit confirmation of their understanding of interactions and situations.
- ☐ show little appreciation for symbolism and metaphors.

Primary Learning Objectives

If you checked any of the identifying behaviors/values for this orientation, determine what your primary learning objectives are and rate the following in order of importance to you. Determine how you might incorporate these objectives into your behavior.

Your challenges may be to:

☐ pay more attention to nonverbal, extra-verbal and overall contextual components of communication and assess them for unexpected or contradictory meaning.

☐ acquire an understanding of the symbolic meaning of cultural components that are operative in a given environment.

☐ try to use more visual cues when communicating with people of a high-context orientation.

Reflection

1. How do you experience this orientation?

2. In which situations do you tend to act on this orientation?

3. Which influences and experiences have shaped your preference?

4. How are the learning objectives relevant to you?

Orientation: Direct

Definition

Social environments that tend to expect, reward and reinforce a **direct** orientation to **communication** emphasize the value of direct and explicit conflict management.

Description

You tend to handle conflict in a direct and explicit manner. You generally see conflict situations as impersonal issues that need to be addressed openly and face-to-face to reach resolution. You believe that conflicts can be positive and constructive and that most can be resolved quickly. Generally, you are not deeply disturbed when tension runs high. You appreciate the benefits of bringing contentious issues into the open. For you, direct conflict management is intricately tied to the notion of honesty and trustworthiness.

When this orientation is strong or very strong, you may:

- not be sufficiently attuned to situations in which it is inappropriate to handle conflict and contentious issues directly.
- be perceived by indirect communicators as insulting, insensitive and lacking intact.
- underestimate the deep sense of embarrassment and "loss of face" that direct confrontation of even presumed conflicts or contentious issues may arouse in indirect communicators.
- feel comfortable giving people feedback shortly after a given task or event.

Following are the identifying behaviors and values of a person with a **direct** orientation to **communication**. Check any boxes corresponding to a behavior you exhibit or a value you hold.

Identifiers

Individuals with this orientation frequently:

- ☐ address problems and conflicts explicitly and immediately.
- ☐ use words to identify and address problems or contentious issues.
- ☐ negatively evaluate indirect ways of managing conflict.

Primary Learning Objectives

If you checked any of the identifying behaviors/values for this orientation, deter-mine what your primary learning objectives are and rate the following in order of importance to you. Determine how you might incorporate these objectives into your behavior.

Challenges for you include:

- ☐ taking care to avoid directly confronting business associates who may be embarrassed by it.
- ☐ increasing your awareness of the situational appropriateness of direct conflict resolution.
- ☐ enhancing your comfort level with the indirect conflict resolution strategies used and preferred by indirect communicators.

Reflection

1. How do you experience this orientation?

2. In which situations do you tend to act on this orientation?

3. Which influences and experiences have shaped your preference?

4. How are the learning objectives relevant to you?

Orientation: Indirect

Definition

Social environments that tend to expect, reward and reinforce an **indirect** orientation to **communication** emphasize the value of indirect and implicit conflict management.

Description

You tend to handle conflict in an implicit way by avoiding direct confrontations. It is important to you to minimize the surface appearance of conflict and criticism. Generally, you see conflict situations as threats to personal integrity, dignity and/or "face."

Preserving and saving "face," personal dignity, and integrity are overriding concerns for you in interactions so as to prevent possible embarrassments. You may prefer passive resistance or the use of formal or informal mediators (lawyers, arbitrators, colleagues, friends, and so on) to address, manage and resolve contentious issues for you. You believe that open conflicts are not beneficial to the parties involved. Openly displayed tensions can disturb you deeply.

When this orientation is strong or very strong, you may:

- project the impression of not having an opinion or wanting to take a stand.

- be approached with suspicion by those who find your indirect style difficult to understand.

- be perceived as dishonest, evasive, weak and fearful by direct communicators.

- prolong existing tensions and negatively affect morale if you refuse to resolve conflict openly.

- reduce or hamper a group's creative and dynamic energy in situations where confronting conflict openly would be an efficient means of releasing it.

- feel feedback is best given via a third-party facilitator or "go between."

Following are the identifying behaviors and values of a person with an **indirect** orientation to **communication**. Check any boxes corresponding to a behavior you exhibit or a value you hold.

Identifiers

Individuals with this orientation frequently:

- ☐ avoid making and addressing critical comments and challenging remarks in public situations.
- ☐ express their true thoughts and feelings about issues and people only to trusted colleagues and friends.
- ☐ implicitly or explicitly expect others to facilitate conflict resolution on their behalf.
- ☐ use implicit, nonverbal, and/or contextual ways to communicate disagreement, frustration and/or anger.

Primary Learning Objectives

If you checked any of the identifying behaviors/values for this orientation, determine what your primary learning objectives are and rate the following in order of importance to you. Determine how you might incorporate these objectives into your behavior.

Your learning challenges include:

- ☐ expressing opinions and sentiments explicitly when appropriate.
- ☐ confronting the parties involved in a problem or conflict.
- ☐ seeing direct communication as beneficial and efficient in certain circumstance.

Reflection

1. How do you experience this orientation?

2. In which situations do you tend to act on this orientation?

3. Which influences and experiences have shaped your preference?

4. How are the learning objectives relevant to you?

Orientation: Expressive

Definition

Social environments that tend to expect, reward and reinforce an **expressive** orientation to **communication** emphasize the value of emotions, eloquence and style in interactions.

Description

As an expressive communicator, you value demonstrative expression in the workplace. In fact, work is an emotional experience for you. Emotional expression and expressiveness play an integral role in convincing and persuading people with whom you work to adopt a particular point of view. It is important for you to see emotional responses to work issues by your counterparts, subordinates and superiors.

You expect both positive and negative emotions to run high in the work environment. You may even require a constant ebb and flow of emotion in order to remain motivated. You tend to be quite animated in your use of words and body language and may even seek and expect physical contact with others. You evaluate the credibility and trustworthiness of coworkers and business partners based on their display of human qualities, which you associate primarily with an open display and expression of emotions.

Style and eloquence may also be critically important to you. You may feel that the display of your personal and professional competence significantly hinges on your ability to express ideas and opinions artfully through the use of similes, metaphors and allegories. Your favorable evaluation of others may be linked to your impression of their stylistic sophistication.

When this orientation is strong or very strong, you may:

- suffer loss of credibility in the eyes of those who evaluate it on the basis of a non-expressive, instrumental or "matter-of-fact" style.

- find that your need for expressiveness and open display of emotions in the workplace can deeply frustrate and demoralize coworkers who are less expressive in their style of communication.

- notice that coworkers with a different orientation may judge your expressive ness and emphasis on eloquence as unprofessional and unbusinesslike.

Following are the identifying behaviors and values of a person with an **expressive** orientation to **communication**. Check any boxes corresponding to a behavior you exhibit or a value you hold.

Identifiers

Individuals with this orientation frequently

- ☐ display positive and negative emotions openly.
- ☐ distinguish themselves through a high degree of empathy.
- ☐ make emotional appeals in order to convince and persuade colleagues and clients that their point of view is correct.
- ☐ appear spontaneous when it is not warranted.
- ☐ use rather complex sentence structures.
- ☐ respond well to metaphors and similes and use them in presentations and/or speeches.

Primary Learning Objectives

If you checked any of the identifying behaviors/values for this orientation, determine what your primary learning objectives are and rate the following in order of importance to you. Determine how you might incorporate these objectives into your behavior.

Some of your challenges will be to:

- ☐ accept emotional detachment in others.
- ☐ restrain your preference for physical contact with people in your work-place.
- ☐ find outlets for the expression of your emotions outside the workplace if they are not considered the norm in the workplace.
- ☐ adjust levels of eloquence and artfulness to an acceptable threshold for your counterparts.
- ☐ tone down the use of emotion in presentations, meetings or one-on-one discussions.

Reflection

1. How do you experience this orientation?

2. In which situations do you tend to act on this orientation?

3. Which influences and experiences have shaped your preference?

4. How are the learning objectives relevant to you?

Orientation: Instrumental

Definition

Social environments that tend to expect, reward and reinforce an **instrumental** orientation to **communication** emphasize the value of accuracy, control and discipline in interactions.

Description

As an instrumental communicator, you value factual, objective and pragmatic exchanges of information. Communication is problem- or issue-centered, impersonal and goal-oriented. You prefer an emotionally detached way of presenting information in order to convince and persuade your coworkers and clients of your perspective on a given matter. You tend to have limited tolerance for displays of emotion in the workplace. Emotional expressiveness in others may cause you to doubt their professionalism, credibility and trustworthiness in business. You often see work relationships as qualitatively different from social relationships, and you evaluate individuals at work on the basis of their direct and measurable contributions to the work at hand.

When this orientation is strong or very strong, you may:

- experience difficulties building rapport and satisfactory interpersonal relationships with those for whom emotional expressiveness is key to determining trustworthiness.

- be perceived as cold, rigid and disconnected or lacking compassion and empathy by those who strongly value emotional expressiveness.

- underestimate the importance of sharing and processing positive as well as negative emotions in the workplace.

Following are the identifying behaviors and values of a person with an **instrumental** orientation to **communication**. Check any boxes corresponding to a behavior you exhibit or a value you hold.

Identifiers

Individuals with this orientation frequently:

- ☐ use a relatively pragmatic and "dry" vocabulary.
- ☐ limit body language in business interactions.
- ☐ get visibly irritated and/or impatient with emotional displays in the workplace.
- ☐ show little appreciation for eloquence of style.

Primary Learning Objectives

If you checked any of the identifying behaviors/values for this orientation, determine what your primary learning objectives are and rate the following in order of importance to you. Determine how you might incorporate these objectives into your behavior.

It will be challenging for you to:

☐ develop an understanding for the emotional needs of coworkers.

☐ build rapport by emotionally connecting with coworkers and business associates.

☐ empathize with others when appropriate in a business environment.

Reflection

1. How do you experience this orientation?

2. In which situations do you tend to act on this orientation?

3. Which influences and experiences have shaped your preference?

4. How are the learning objectives relevant to you?

Orientation: Formal

Definition

Social environments that tend to expect, reward and reinforce a **formal** orientation to **communication** emphasize the importance of following protocol and social customs.

Description

It is important to you to observe specific rules of etiquette and protocol in the workplace and in business situations. This need is particularly strong in your interactions with superiors. Likewise, you expect subordinates to be mindful of etiquette when interacting with you. You feel that observing decorum establishes credibility, respect and sincerity.

Overall, you see formalities, social conventions and customs as conducive to communication as well as to the development of business and social relationships. You feel uncomfortable in informal business environments and may perceive informality as communicating a lack of respect for you, your position and your endeavors. You see a lack of formality in others as indicative of their lack of professionalism, education and social graces. You tend to be keenly aware of the social structures within which you operate. You value respectful interactions.

When this orientation is strong or very strong, you may:

- be perceived as rigid and distant by people who expect a more flexible and informal approach.

- prefer conservative business clothing.

- have difficulty overcoming your aversion to informal speech, clothing, manners, and forms of address in order to conduct the business at hand.

- feel alienated when working in an informal social environment.

Following are the identifying behaviors and values of a person with a **formal** orientation to **communication**. Check any boxes corresponding to a behavior you exhibit or a value you hold.

Identifiers

Individuals with this orientation frequently:

- ☐ carry an aura of seriousness into the workplace and business interactions.
- ☐ dress according to formal, conservative, or traditional conventions of the social environment.
- ☐ refrain from using colloquial language and adhere to rules of grammar.
- ☐ are sensitive to proper forms of address.

Primary Learning Objectives

If you checked any of the identifying behaviors/values for this orientation, determine what your primary learning objectives are and rate the following in order of importance to you. Determine how you might incorporate these objectives into your behavior.

Your learning challenges are to:

- ☐ understand the value of informality.
- ☐ increase your comfort level with informal interactions.
- ☐ learn to extend yourself on a personal level when warranted.

Reflection

1. How do you experience this orientation?

2. In which situations do you tend to act on this orientation?

3. Which influences and experiences have shaped your preference?

4. How are the learning objectives relevant to you?

Orientation: Informal

Definition

Social environments that tend to expect, reward and reinforce an **informal** orientation to **communication** emphasize the importance of dispensing with ceremony and protocol.

Description

You value casual, relaxed and friendly conduct in the workplace and in business situations. You find that observing etiquette, decorum, and tradition establishes an undesirable distance between people. For you, credibility, trustworthiness and sincerity are intricately tied to a friendly, casual and jovial style.

You see formalities, social conventions, and customs as unnecessary and as insurmountable barriers to good communication and solving problems. You are uncomfortable in formal situations and feel alienated and excluded by those who maintain social distance from you through the use of rules and decorum. You may feel uncomfortable when participating in traditional customs and rituals.

You tend to value a free, open, and uncensored flow of opinions and thoughts. You emphasize flexibility and spontaneity and an appearance of basic equality between the people in a business relationship.

When this orientation is strong or very strong, you may:

- be perceived as rude, unpolished, and disrespectful by those who value formal communication.

- unknowingly take away a necessary foundation for maintaining satisfactory communication if you unwittingly engage in informal communication with people for whom adherence to protocol and social conventions is essential.

- inadvertently and inappropriately transgress relationship boundaries (for example, speak to someone as if he or she were a close friend rather than a business acquaintance).

Following are the identifying behaviors and values of a person with an **informal** orientation to **communication**. Check any boxes corresponding to a behavior you exhibit or a value you hold.

Identifiers

Individuals with this orientation frequently:

- ☐ are clearly unconcerned with protocol and etiquette.
- ☐ appear uncomfortable in situations that require adhering to rules of decorum and protocol.
- ☐ exhibit a desire to feel comfortable and relaxed in business situations.

Primary Learning Objectives

If you checked any of the identifying behaviors/values for this orientation, determine what your primary learning objectives are and rate the following in order of importance to you. Determine how you might incorporate these objectives into your behavior.

Your challenges will be to:

- ☐ increase your comfort level with formality and social distance.
- ☐ understand the usefulness, value and social significance of formal ways of behaving in a business situation.
- ☐ familiarize yourself with the rules of etiquette and protocol in particular social environments.

Reflection

1. How do you experience this orientation?

2. In which situations do you tend to act on this orientation?

3. Which influences and experiences have shaped your preference?

4. How are the learning objectives relevant to you?

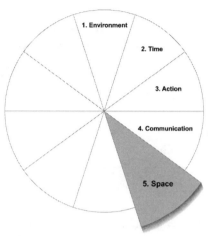

Dimension: Space

How individuals establish their physical and psychological space.

Orientation: Private

Definition

People with a private **space** orientation generally prefer to put greater distance between themselves and others, and physical contact is limited.

Description

Private-space cultures may place distance between people through separate offices, seating arrangements, or the size of the room. Private-space cultures place an emphasis on closed-door meetings with minimal interruptions. People prefer to stand farther apart and tend not to touch during conversation. Private space-oriented people prefer a task-oriented approach to communicating with others and select locations that enhance their ability to problem solve and reach agreement. The use of technology for communication may be expected and emphasized for sharing information across long distances. Private-space cultures may require more de-centralization and empowerment of individuals because managers cannot supervise the daily activities of subordinates who are separated.

Private and public orientations to space can also lead to a distinction between what information can be shared or not shared among members of a group. People with a private-space orientation tend to share information on a "need to know" basis. Office spaces that separate people and job tasks may lead to less information sharing, even if everyone is connected electronically.

When this orientation is strong or very strong, you may:

- appear shy, withdrawn, disengaged and/or disinterested to people with the opposite orientation.

- be seen as unduly secretive and therefore to be distrusted by people with the opposite orientation.

- be perceived as inaccessible and unapproachable by public-space-oriented coworkers and business associates.

Orientation: Private

Following are the identifying behaviors and values of a person with a **private** orientation to **space**. Check any boxes corresponding to a behavior you exhibit or a value you hold.

Identifiers

Individuals with this orientation frequently:

- ☐ spend time by themselves and seek seclusion.
- ☐ avoid close proximity to and physical contact with others.
- ☐ clearly establish physical boundaries in the work environment.
- ☐ apologize when intruding on the space of another (as in "I'm sorry to disturb you").
- ☐ feel a need to schedule appointments with people who work in their immediate vicinity in order to avoid disturbing them unexpectedly.
- ☐ share information on a need-to-know basis.

Primary Learning Objectives

If you checked any of the identifying behaviors/values for this orientation, determine what your primary learning objectives are and rate the following in order of importance to you. Determine how you might incorporate these objectives into your behavior.

Some of your challenges are to:

- ☐ stop yourself from expressing frustration and anger when coworkers enter your work area.
- ☐ feel more comfortable in social situations and public environments.
- ☐ learn to disclose information more freely and openly when appropriate.
- ☐ establish a greater comfort level with contextually appropriate physical contact with and proximity to others.

Reflection

1. How do you experience this orientation?

2. In which situations do you tend to act on this orientation?

3. Which influences and experiences have shaped your preference?

4. How are the learning objectives relevant to you?

Orientation: Public

Definition

People with a **public** orientation generally prefer to put less distance between themselves and others. Physical contact is common and expected, even between people of different genders.

Description

Office space in public-space cultures may seem small, crowded and noisy. Public-space cultures place an emphasis on open-door meetings and are comfortable with frequent interruptions. People prefer to stand closer together and tend to touch when communicating. Public space-oriented people prefer a relationship-oriented approach to communicating with others and select locations that enhance the development of trust and rapport. The use of technology, while utilized for communication, may not replace the need for face-to-face meetings or the informal exchange of information between people. Public-space cultures may establish control over larger office spaces through the centralization of work activities and decision making, which ensures that performance and progress can be monitored.

Private and public orientations to space can also lead to a distinction between what information can be shared or not shared among members of a group. Public orientations tend to share information on a "nice to know" basis with those members who belong to their work or social group. Office spaces that group people together in one large room and require daily interaction and a sharing of resources can lead to more information being shared among members.

When this orientation is strong or very strong, you may:

- be perceived as intrusive by individuals with a private-space orientation.
- find that others view your expectation of disclosure and information sharing as inappropriate.
- transgress important social boundaries and therefore be treated without respect in the workplace.
- offend others when you had intended to express something positive.
- be seen as naïve by others who may take advantage of your openness in disclosing information.
- frequently seek closeness with business associates.

Following are the identifying behaviors and values of a person with a **public** orientation to **space**. Check any boxes corresponding to a behavior you exhibit or a value you hold.

Identifiers

Individuals with this orientation frequently:

- ☐ engage in physical contact (touching, embracing and so forth).
- ☐ seek out public social environments.
- ☐ stand close to others when interacting with them.

Primary Learning Objectives

If you checked any of the identifying behaviors/values for this orientation, determine what your primary learning objectives are and rate the following in order of importance to you. Determine how you might incorporate these objectives into your behavior.

Your learning challenges are to:

- ☐ develop the skill of gradually disclosing information.
- ☐ understand the markers that distinguish public from private domains and behaviors.
- ☐ be comfortable with distance in an interaction.
- ☐ avoid physical contact, especially with subordinates who may not feel comfortable expressing discomfort with such contact.

Reflection

1. How do you experience this orientation?

2. In which situations do you tend to act on this orientation?

3. Which influences and experiences have shaped your preference?

4. How are the learning objectives relevant to you?

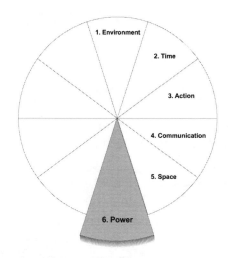

Dimension: Power

How individuals view differential power relationships.

Orientation: Hierarchy

Definition

Social environments that tend to expect, reward and reinforce a **hierarchy** orientation place a high premium on power structures and the recognition of power and status differentials among individuals.

Description

You assume that society and organizations must be stratified in order to function properly. As a result, you assume that everyone has a qualitatively different value, as well as different rights and responsibilities. Title, rank, position and/or age bestow authority and status on individuals who must be respected by people in lower ranks.

You may feel it is important to show respect and deference openly and acknowledge "power distance" by using appropriate forms of address that reinforce hierarchical structures and social status. For you, it is not acceptable to bypass formal lines of authority in order to complete a task.

You prefer to work in organizations that maintain demarcated lines of power and authority and where work is performed according to the specifications of superiors. You require clear job descriptions that indicate detailed performance expectations.

When this orientation is strong or very strong, you may:

- seem overly status conscious, pompous, or pretentious and alienate those who have an egalitarian view of social relations.

- feel alienated and have difficulties establishing rapport in an egalitarian environment.

- be shown no respect by people who do not share your emphasis on hierarchy and status.

- ignore the fact that, for equality-oriented individuals, respect must be earned over time and is not inherent in a position, function or educational level.

Following are the identifying behaviors and values of a person with a **hierarchy** orientation to **power**. Check any boxes corresponding to a behavior you exhibit or a value you hold.

Identifiers

Individuals with this orientation frequently:

- ☐ surround themselves with objects that connote status and power.
- ☐ tell a superior what he/she wants to hear, not what they really think.
- ☐ emphasize and display evidence of their educational achievements.
- ☐ use declarative or imperative expressions.
- ☐ do not contradict a superior publicly or privately.
- ☐ refrain from offering personal opinions about key decisions to a superior.
- ☐ express outrage when coworkers behave in ways that show disrespect for higher status or position.

Primary Learning Objectives

If you checked any of the identifying behaviors/values for this orientation, determine what your primary learning objectives are and rate the following in order of importance to you. Determine how you might incorporate these objectives into your behavior.

You may find it a challenge to:

- ☐ understand the psychological role of an equality orientation in the workplace.
- ☐ develop coping mechanisms when you feel undervalued or disrespected by equality-oriented individuals.
- ☐ learn how respect is acquired and communicated in interactions in a given equality-oriented environment.
- ☐ learn to share opinions freely and honestly with peers and superiors.
- ☐ de-emphasize the importance you place on status and/or educational achievements.

Reflection

1. How do you experience this orientation?

2. In which situations do you tend to act on this orientation?

3. Which influences and experiences have shaped your preference?

4. How are the learning objectives relevant to you?

Orientation: Equality

Definition

Social environments that tend to expect, reward and reinforce an **equality** orientation minimize power structures in an organization and emphasize the equality of status among individuals.

Description

You assume that everyone has the same essential value, rights, responsibilities and social status. You tend to downplay, minimize or even hide economic and social differences both at work and in your personal life. It is important to you that everyone is included and has the same opportunities. You tend to be sensitive to the needs of everyone in a situation.

It is acceptable for you to bypass formal lines of authority in order to get things done. You may also feel uneasy with and irritated by official titles and forms of address that reinforce hierarchical structures. You generally prefer to work within a "flat" organizational structure.

When this orientation is strong or very strong, you may:

☐ not notice that others expect you to maintain an appropriate "power distance" due to their elevated status and position.

☐ cause confusion in hierarchy-oriented individuals who may interpret your behavior as unwarranted "fraternization."

☐ be perceived as lacking a clear understanding of your status and role.

☐ be seen as rude and disrespectful or lacking in social graces.

☐ create great conflict and consternation in hierarchy-oriented individuals who report to you and may not understand your attempts to "empower" them.

☐ have difficulty assuming a position of status and authority even when it is expected of you.

Following are the identifying behaviors and values of a person with an **equality** orientation to **power**. Check any boxes corresponding to a behavior you exhibit or a value you hold.

Identifiers

Individuals with this orientation frequently:

- ☐ use open-ended questions when making requests of subordinates.
- ☐ downplay their own and ignore others' formal titles.
- ☐ start relationships informally.
- ☐ stress that everyone's opinion is valued.
- ☐ display irritation or even outrage when observing deferential or status-conscious behavior.
- ☐ feel comfortable contradicting superiors publicly and privately.
- ☐ offer personal opinions about key decisions to a superior.

Primary Learning Objectives

If you checked any of the identifying behaviors/values for this orientation, determine what your primary learning objectives are and rate the following in order of importance to you. Determine how you might incorporate these objectives into your behavior.

Your challenges are to:

- ☐ consider the impact of your decisions and actions on others in the work environment.
- ☐ understand the needs of those who identify with and are motivated by collective undertakings.
- ☐ increase tolerance for situations in which individual choices are absent and matters are socially determined.
- ☐ de-emphasize self-interest and consider group or team interests more seriously.

Reflection

1. How do you experience this orientation?

2. In which situations do you tend to act on this orientation?

3. Which influences and experiences have shaped your preference?

4. How are the learning objectives relevant to you?

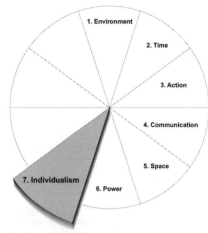

Dimension: Individualism

How individuals define their identify.

Orientation: Individualistic

Definition

Social environments that tend to expect, reward and reinforce an **individualistic** orientation emphasize individual motivation and personal independence and achievement as the cornerstones of identity.

Description

You are driven and motivated primarily by your own personal interests, accomplishments and potentials. You make decisions and take action according to what is best for you, based on your own wishes and judgment. You require and expect your environment to provide you with a great degree of personal choice.

You expect every individual to be primarily responsible for him- or herself. You see the value of conflict between individuals as the natural way in which they assert their personal interests, reach their goals and meet their needs.

You value personal independence, prize individual achievements and you expect to be recognized and rewarded for your own contributions and achievements. You value and admire self-driven, determined and self-motivated individuals.

When this orientation is strong or very strong, you may:

- ☐ seem selfish and inconsiderate of others.
- ☐ often underestimate the need for groups to process information.
- ☐ tend to ignore or overlook the productive potential of a cohesive group.
- ☐ experience difficulties working effectively in teams.
- ☐ alienate those who are primarily motivated by collaborative efforts.
- ☐ become frustrated and irritated with an absence of choices.

Following are the identifying behaviors and values of a person with an **individualistic** orientation to **individualism**. Check any boxes corresponding to a behavior you exhibit or a value you hold.

Identifiers

Individuals with this orientation frequently:

- ☐ discuss themselves and their motivation and interests.
- ☐ emphasize the first person singular when proposing ideas (e.g., "I think...").
- ☐ act and make decisions without informing or preparing others.
- ☐ decrease their interest in and contribution to activities when the personal benefits become less obvious to them.
- ☐ do not display consideration of the impact of their decisions and actions on others.
- ☐ view teams as a temporary collection of individuals.
- ☐ resist and object to predetermined structures and processes.
- ☐ maintain a loose relationship to others in their larger social environment.

Primary Learning Objectives

If you checked any of the identifying behaviors/values for this orientation, determine what your primary learning objectives are and rate the following in order of importance to you. Determine how you might incorporate these objectives into your behavior.

Your challenges are to:

- ☐ consider the impact of your decisions and actions on others in the work environment.
- ☐ understand the needs of those who identify with and are motivated by collective undertakings.
- ☐ increase tolerance for situations in which individual choices are absent and matters are socially determined.
- ☐ de-emphasize self-interest and consider group or team interests more seriously.

Reflection

1. How do you experience this orientation?

2. In which situations do you tend to act on this orientation?

3. Which influences and experiences have shaped your preference?

4. How are the learning objectives relevant to you?

Orientation: Collectivistic

Definition

Social environments that tend to expect, reward and reinforce a **collectivistic** orientation place a high value on the subordination of individual interests to those of a group and emphasize group membership as a defining characteristic of identity.

Description

You are motivated and driven primarily by your affiliation with groups and/or organizations. You make decisions according to what is best for your organization and determine actions based on its expectations of you. You prefer to make decisions by building group consensus, and you expect groups and organizations to take care of their constituents. You tend to experience open conflict as negative and disruptive to group functioning and you avoid and or minimize any potential for its occurrence. You value close interdependence and prize the accomplishments of groups. You are uncomfortable in situations in which you are isolated from the group, individually rewarded for your efforts or have to make decisions by yourself. You have a strong sense of loyalty to your chosen organizations. You assimilate corporate/organizational goals and characteristics as your own, and you have a strong sense of social responsibility and obligation.

When this orientation is strong or very strong, you may:

- frustrate those who expect you to recognize their individual contributions and skills.
- seem overly dependent on others and lacking in individual assertiveness to those who expect you to take individual initiative.
- be easily frustrated and flustered by a superior or corporate environment that emphasizes individual accountability and decision making.
- dislike environments in which performance is measured on an individual basis.

Following are the identifying behaviors and values of a person with a **collectivistic** orientation to **individualism**. Check any boxes corresponding to a behavior you exhibit or a value you hold.

Identifiers

Individuals with this orientation frequently:

- ☐ require meetings to process information and make decisions.
- ☐ do not determine an action quickly or by themselves.
- ☐ seek feedback from others.
- ☐ feel personally offended when the group or organization is criticized.
- ☐ show great concern for the impact of decisions and events on the group/organization.

- ☐ use the first person plural when referring to business processes, accomplishments and goals.
- ☐ defend decisions made by their group, even if they personally had no role in the decisions.
- ☐ view themselves as a permanent extension of a group/organization and expect security from the organization while offering loyalty in return.

Primary Learning Objectives

If you checked any of the identifying behaviors/values for this orientation, determine what your primary learning objectives are and rate the following in order of importance to you Determine how you might incorporate these objectives into your behavior.

You may find it a challenge to:

- ☐ feel comfortable doing something based on personal motives or only in your own interest.
- ☐ make decisions by yourself.
- ☐ assert your own opinion.
- ☐ put your interests before those of the group.
- ☐ be held individually accountable for a given project.

Reflection

1. How do you experience this orientation?

2. In which situations do you tend to act on this orientation?

3. Which influences and experiences have shaped your preference?

4. How are the learning objectives relevant to you?

Orientation: Universalistic

Definition

Social environments that tend to expect, reward, and reinforce a **universalistic** orientation place a high value on standards, procedures, rules and laws and emphasize the equal rights and responsibilities of individuals and/or groups.

Description

Your judgments and actions are guided by an abstract sense of fairness and right and wrong. You value the equal application of standard rules, principles and processes. You believe that everyone has essentially the same rights and responsibilities regardless of particular circumstances. Your sense of obligation is primarily tied to rules and not to individuals.

You dislike favoritism and value fairness as an essential component of integrity and professionalism. You expect people to adhere to general guidelines.

When this orientation is strong or very strong, you may:

- be perceived as mechanistic, bureaucratic, and rigid by those with a particularistic orientation.

- alienate people who expect special and individual consideration.

Following are the identifying behaviors and values of a person with a **universalistic** orientation to **individualism**. Check any boxes corresponding to a behavior you exhibit or a value you hold.

Identifiers

Individuals with this orientation frequently:

- ☐ refer to universally applicable rules, standards and principles when assessing situations.
- ☐ seek to establish rules and processes when solving problems.
- ☐ resort to formalized problem resolution (e.g., lawsuits).
- ☐ expect consistent behavior from others in a wide range of situations.
- ☐ strongly believe that there is one "truth" and/or one "right way."

Primary Learning Objectives

If you checked any of the identifying behaviors/values for this orientation, determine what your primary learning objectives are and rate the following in order of importance to you. Determine how you might incorporate these objectives into your behavior.

Your challenges may be to:

- ☐ develop a greater sensitivity to the different needs in various situations.
- ☐ meet the interactive needs of those who require affirmation of their uniqueness.
- ☐ understand the needs of business associates with a particularistic orientation.

Reflection

1. How do you experience this orientation?

2. In which situations do you tend to act on this orientation?

3. Which influences and experiences have shaped your preference?

4. How are the learning objectives relevant to you?

Orientation: Particularistic

Definition

Social environments that tend to expect, reward and reinforce a **particularistic** orientation value the difference and uniqueness of individuals and/or groups and emphasize the differential applicability of rules and procedures.

Description

Your sense of obligation centers primarily around your family and social network. You have a strong sense of your own uniqueness. Trust in and obligation to those in your network tend to determine your decisions. You are very loyal to the people in your network and expect loyalty from them in return.

You may respect formal rules and procedures for conduct but tend to think they do not apply to you. You value and encourage uniqueness and the careful consideration of particular circumstances. You tend to view norms, rules, and procedures as expressions of intent and as loose guidelines, but you may not feel bound by them. You value the ability to adapt your behavior and approach to the requirements of the situation.

When this orientation is strong or very strong, you may:

- be perceived as disrespectful and obstructionist because you refuse or seem to refuse to comply with norms and rules.

- be viewed as eccentric by people who are universalistic in orientation.

- be seen as showing favoritism if you change or bend the rules for particular individuals.

- be regarded as unfair by those who do not share your orientation.

Identifiers

Individuals with this orientation frequently:

- ☐ emphasize the unique and particular circumstances of a given situation.
- ☐ make exceptions to norms, rules or procedures.
- ☐ expect that rules and norms do not apply to them.
- ☐ accentuate their uniqueness through unconventional behaviors and/or accessories.
- ☐ visibly display their membership in a particular group.
- ☐ believe that there are multiple truths and a variety of acceptable ways of doing things.

Primary Learning Objectives

If you checked any of the identifying behaviors/values for this orientation, determine what your primary learning objectives are and rate the following in order of importance to you. Determine how you might incorporate these objectives into your behavior.

Your learning challenges may be to:

☐ place trust in standards, procedures and rules.

☐ meet the interactive needs of those who require an affirmation of uniform standards and formalized problem resolution.

☐ operate according to rules in a universalistic business environment.

Reflection

1. How do you experience this orientation?

2. In which situations do you tend to act on this orientation?

3. Which influences and experiences have shaped your preference?

4. How are the learning objectives relevant to you?

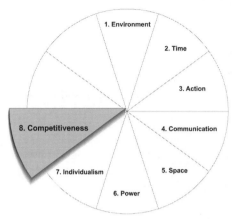

Dimension: Competitiveness

How individuals are motivated.

Orientation: Competitive

Definition

Social environments that tend to expect, reward, and reinforce a competitive orientation value achievement, assertiveness and material success. The expected outcomes and projected results of interactions are primary motivators.

Description

You generally assume that employees compete for recognition and rewards. You value achievement and results. Personal ambition and assertiveness are important to you. Harmonious teamwork, consensus building and the development of mutually beneficial interdependencies are not powerful motivators for your behavior and actions.

When this orientation is strong or very strong, you may:

- have a clearly defined sense of your personal strengths and contributions to the workplace.

- be very comfortable articulating and defending a personal opinion and expect others to do likewise.

- often take full responsibility for your performance.

- have difficulty extending trust to others.

- be perceived as too aggressive and confrontational by less competitive individuals.

- underestimate the need of those with a strong cooperative orientation for harmonious and trusting team and workplace relationships.

Following are the identifying behaviors and values of a person with a **competitive** orientation to **competitiveness**. Check any boxes corresponding to a behavior you exhibit or a value you hold.

Identifiers

Individuals with this orientation frequently:

- ☐   assert their opinions and desires.
- ☐   emphasize achievement, results and goals.
- ☐   display and underscore achievement through material possessions and personal accessories.

Primary Learning Objectives

If you checked any of the identifying behaviors/values for this orientation, determine what your primary learning objectives are and rate the following in order of importance to you. Determine how you might incorporate these objectives into your behavior.

Your learning challenges may be to:

- ☐   trust individuals, groups, and team processes.
- ☐   take into account the impact of your goals and needs on others in the work-place.
- ☐   become less confrontational when appropriate.
- ☐   develop an appreciation for consensus building.

Reflection

1. How do you experience this orientation?

2. In which situations do you tend to act on this orientation?

3. Which influences and experiences have shaped your preference?

4. How are the learning objectives relevant to you?

Orientation: Cooperative

Definition

Social environments that tend to expect, reward and reinforce a **cooperative** orientation value interdependence. The quality of relationships and interactions is a primary motivator.

Description

You seek harmonious and mutually supportive, even familial, relationships with colleagues and coworkers; you expect to build strong and trusting relationships with them. It is important to you to maintain and nurture long-term relationships built on trust. You tend to be strongly team- and group-oriented and place great value on conforming with established norms, patterns and procedures.

When this orientation is strong or very strong, you may:

- avoid openly competitive and aggressive situations.
- be easily discouraged and frustrated by colleagues who see themselves in personal competition with you or other colleagues.
- be perceived as lacking self-confidence and conviction by individuals with a competitive orientation.

Following are the identifying behaviors and values of a person with a **cooperative** orientation to **competitiveness**. Check any boxes corresponding to a behavior you exhibit or a value you hold.

Identifiers

Individuals with this orientation frequently:

- ☐ emphasize the importance of process and balance.
- ☐ spend a lot of time building and maintaining relationships.
- ☐ avoid behaviors that make them conspicuous or that call attention to them in any way.
- ☐ seek consensus in decision making.

Primary Learning Objectives

If you checked any of the identifying behaviors/values for this orientation, determine what your primary learning objectives are and rate the following in order of importance to you. Determine how you might incorporate these objectives into your behavior.

Your challenges may be to:

- ☐ make decisions without building a consensus first, when warranted.
- ☐ express yourself in ways that communicate self-confidence.
- ☐ enter into competitive situations more easily.
- ☐ define your personal needs, goals and ambitions before entering a competitive business environment.

Reflection

1. How do you experience this orientation?

2. In which situations do you tend to act on this orientation?

3. Which influences and experiences have shaped your preference?

4. How are the learning objectives relevant to you?

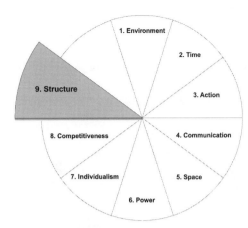

Dimension: Structure

How individuals approach change, risk, ambiguity and uncertainty.

Orientation: Order

Definition

Social environments that tend to expect, reward and reinforce an **order** orientation value stability, predictability and the avoidance of risks.

Description

You tend to feel comfortable with clearly defined parameters and guidelines for action and work activities. You prefer a precisely defined job description that explicitly states what is expected of you. You expect the work environment to be stable. You value rules, regulations, and systematic procedures that are consistently applied. Predictability and security are appealing to you. You tend to feel threatened by irregularities, uncertainty and change. Your need to avoid risk and seek predictability and stability guides your decision making and problem solving.

When this orientation is strong or very strong, you may:

- be perceived as inflexible and obstructionist in situations in which others accept change and adaptability as the norm.

- be viewed as reactive and timid by those who value flexibility.

- seem overly concerned with internal matter — such as systematizing, organizing, and structuring — to the exclusion of external business considerations.

Following are the identifying behaviors and values of a person with an **order** orientation to **structure**. Check any boxes corresponding to a behavior you exhibit or a value you hold.

Identifiers

Individuals with this orientation frequently

- ☐ emphasize the need for stability, consistency, predictability and the containment of risk.
- ☐ require a lot of information, data, and time for contemplation in order to make decisions.
- ☐ create elaborate contingency plans.
- ☐ create and look to rules, systems and structures as solutions to problems.
- ☐ are irritated, insecure, and frustrated in situations that are unpredictable or ambiguous or that require improvisation and spontaneity.
- ☐ resist and avoid change.

Primary Learning Objectives

If you checked any of the identifying behaviors/values for this orientation, determine what your primary learning objectives are and rate the following in order of importance to you. Determine how you might incorporate these objectives into your behavior.

Your challenges may be to:

- ☐ increase comfort with change in environments that are very dynamic.
- ☐ feel more comfortable with unknown quantities and unpredictable events.
- ☐ improvise and take advantage of the creativity spontaneity offers.

Reflection

1. How do you experience this orientation?

2. In which situations do you tend to act on this orientation?

3. Which influences and experiences have shaped your preference?

4. How are the learning objectives relevant to you?

Orientation: Flexibility

Definition

Social environments that tend to expect, reward and reinforce a **flexibility** orientation value change, risk taking and adaptability to unfamiliar circumstances.

Description

You expect the conditions of your work to change and are willing to adjust your behavior, activities and priorities accordingly. You value innovative and unconventional ways of doing things and are open to new behavior patterns. You tend to view change and risk as opportunities for growth. You are not threatened by shifting parameters or unpredictable and ambiguous situations. You are comfortable in situations that require you to take risks, improvise or be spontaneous. You tend to value and strive for innovation and adaptability.

When this orientation is strong or very strong, you may:

- strongly resist settling into routines and structures and underestimate their importance in team- and group-oriented work situations.

- be perceived as insensitive to the profound stress that change and risk can produce iorder-oriented individuals.

Following are the identifying behaviors and values of a person with a **flexibility** orientation to **structure**. Check any boxes corresponding to a behavior you exhibit or a value you hold.

Identifiers

Individuals with this orientation frequently:

- ☐ de-emphasize the need for detailed preparation before meetings, presentations and negotiations.
- ☐ trust their ability to "make things work" without much preparation.
- ☐ emphasize the positive nature of risk and change.
- ☐ seek out innovation and new, unconventional ways of doing things.
- ☐ challenge the status quo.

Primary Learning Objectives

If you checked any of the identifying behaviors/values for this orientation, determine what your primary learning objectives are and rate the following in order of importance to you. Determine how you might incorporate these objectives into your behavior.

Your challenges may be to:

- ☐ increase comfort with ordered and structured environments.
- ☐ understand the need for stability and predictability in order-oriented individuals.
- ☐ lower expectations for a quick pace and speedy changes when working with order-oriented individuals.
- ☐ accept that order-oriented individuals require more time and preparation in order to make change and innovation possible.
- ☐ understand the value to others of preparing for events.
- ☐ accept the status quo when it is advisable or beneficial to you.

Reflection

1. How do you experience this orientation?

2. In which situations do you tend to act on this orientation?

3. Which influences and experiences have shaped your preference?

4. How are the learning objectives relevant to you?

Dimension: Thinking

How individuals conceptualize.

Orientation: Inductive

Definition

Social environments that tend to expect, reward and reinforce an **inductive** orientation value reasoning based on experience, particular incidents and experimentation.

Description

You are interested in the details and particular components of situations and circumstances. In other words, you emphasize the specific over the general. You expect patterns and principles to emerge from situations and readily assume that they will serve as rough guides in planning actions and activities. You are generally detail-oriented and emphasize the careful analysis and interpretation of data. Abstract theories and principles mean relatively little to you if they do not emerge from individual circumstances and do not support a pragmatic approach to handling issues.

When this orientation is strong or very strong, you may:

- be perceived as lost in the details to the exclusion of sound principles and theories.
- underestimate the utility of theories, principles and processes.
- get impatient and frustrated by theories and deductive arguments or presentations.
- be viewed by deductive thinkers as lacking principles and convictions.

Following are the identifying behaviors and values of a person with an **inductive** orientation to **thinking**. Check any boxes corresponding to a behavior you exhibit or a value you hold.

Identifiers

Individuals with this orientation frequently:

- ☐ focus and comment on the details of a situation.
- ☐ are interested in discussing case studies rather than theories.
- ☐ emphasize application.
- ☐ get impatient with discussions of abstract theories and principles.
- ☐ ask for examples to illustrate a given idea.

Primary Learning Objectives

If you checked any of the identifying behaviors/values for this orientation, determine what your primary learning objectives are and rate the following in order of importance to you. Determine how you might incorporate these objectives into your behavior.

Your learning challenges may be to:

- ☐ appreciate the utility of theories and abstract concepts.
- ☐ develop patience with a deductive approach to planning, decision making and problem solving.

Reflection

1. How do you experience this orientation?

2. In which situations do you tend to act on this orientation?

3. Which influences and experiences have shaped your preference?

4. How are the learning objectives relevant to you?

Orientation: Deductive

Definition

Social environments that tend to expect, reward and reinforce a **deductive** orientation value reasoning based on principles, theories and abstract logic.

Description

You focus primarily on theories, abstract concepts, and principles rather than on the details of a situation. In other words, your thinking moves from the general to the specific. You tend to evaluate the quality and soundness of a presentation or a proposal based on the concepts upon which they rest. You get frustrated when the conceptual foundation is not readily apparent or sufficiently developed. You tend to scrutinize and debate conceptual frameworks and key principles before applying them to individual situations. In addition, you frequently introduce new ideas by outlining and discussing the underlying principles and theories rather than their application to particular scenarios.

When this orientation is strong or very strong, you may:

- be perceived as unrealistic or lost in conceptualization and abstraction by people who do not value this orientation.

- focus on scrutinizing theories, thereby neglecting the particular situation under consideration.

- ignore significant particulars in order to "fit" data to a theory.

- be perceived as dogmatic and inflexible by inductive thinkers.

Following are the identifying behaviors and values of a person with a **deductive** orientation to **thinking**. Check any boxes corresponding to a behavior you exhibit or a value you hold.

Identifiers

Individuals with this orientation frequently:

- ☐ comment on, critique, and question the soundness of theories on an abstract level.
- ☐ present theories, concepts, and models before describing particular cases.
- ☐ de-emphasize application and implementation.
- ☐ get impatient and frustrated with case studies and anecdotes.

Primary Learning Objectives

If you checked any of the identifying behaviors/values for this orientation, determine what your primary learning objectives are and rate the following in order of importance to you. Determine how you might incorporate these objectives into your behavior.

Your learning challenges may be to:

☐ resist "fitting" data to a theory.

☐ pay greater attention to detail.

☐ focus on the application and implementation of concepts and models.

☐ learn to value case studies and anecdotes in some contexts.

Reflection

1. How do you experience this orientation?

2. In which situations do you tend to act on this orientation?

3. Which influences and experiences have shaped your preference?

4. How are the learning objectives relevant to you?

Orientation: Linear

Definition

Social environments that tend to expect, reward and reinforce a **linear** orientation focus on the sequential and isolated consideration of issues and ideas.

Description

You prefer to approach issues and problems from an analytical perspective. A holistic, systemic presentation of problems and issues can be very frustrating for you. You tend to look for ways to identify discrete components and map primary cause-and-effect relationships. You prefer to convert issues into causal chains of events, each of which can be handled as an individual entity. You tend to articulate ideas, present proposals, and convince others by presenting each variable individually and in a logically determined sequence. You assess the ideas of others based on analytical and logical soundness and get frustrated when these criteria are absent.

When this orientation is strong or very strong, you may:

- be quite pragmatic and concerned with analytic soundness.
- focus on actionable components.
- be able to concentrate on the details of individual variables.
- be frustrated and sometimes even "paralyzed" by complexity or systemic thinking.
- have a tendency to overemphasize the details of individual components to the exclusion of the goal of the entirety.
- feel frustrated by what appears to be an inability to conceptualize the relationships between and among components or issues.

Following are the identifying behaviors and values of a person with a **linear** orientation to **thinking**. Check any boxes corresponding to a behavior you exhibit or a value you hold.

Identifiers

Individuals with this orientation frequently:

- ☐ find the arguments of systemic thinkers lacking in focus and clarity.
- ☐ structure presentations by outlining discrete components and sequentially treating each one.

Primary Learning Objectives

If you checked any of the identifying behaviors/values for this orientation, determine what your primary learning objectives are and rate the following in order of importance to you. Determine how you might incorporate these objectives into your behavior.

Your learning challenges may be to:

☐ focus on the "big picture" as well as the discrete components of a process.

☐ practice a more synthetic way of conceptualizing.

Reflection

1. How do you experience this orientation?

2. In which situations do you tend to act on this orientation?

3. Which influences and experiences have shaped your preference?

4. How are the learning objectives relevant to you?

Orientation: Systemic

Definition

Social environments that tend to expect, reward and reinforce a **systemic** orientation focus on the holistic interrelatedness and integration of issues and ideas.

Description

You prefer to approach questions and problems from a broad, "big picture" perspective. You tend to focus on relationships between concepts or components of a situation. In order to persuade others to accept a proposition or argument, you point out the likely impact and effect on related variables. You prefer a synthetic pattern of thinking. Being mindful of the complexity and interrelatedness of issues is a hallmark of realism for you. You tend to find a linear orientation to thinking reductionist and naïve.

When this orientation is strong or very strong, you may:

- tend to present issues in a complex way that can seem clumsy and convoluted to individuals with a linear orientation.

- overemphasize the "big picture" and overlook important details.

- feel stifled or paralyzed by the complexity of issues before you.

Following are the identifying behaviors and values of a person with a **systemic** orientation to **thinking**. Check any boxes corresponding to a behavior you exhibit or a value you hold.

Identifiers

Individuals with this orientation frequently:

☐ focus and comment on the interrelatedness of issues.

☐ emphasize the complexity of issues and their theoretical ramifications.

☐ find linear approaches overly simplistic.

☐ structure presentations in a synthetic way by emphasizing complex interconnections between issues.

Primary Learning Experience

If you checked any of the identifying behaviors/values for this orientation, determine what your primary learning objectives are and rate the following in order of importance to you. Determine how you might incorporate these objectives into your behavior.

Your learning challenges may be to:

☐ develop greater appreciation for and patience with a linear approach.

☐ develop a more analytic approach to conceptualization.

Reflection

1. How do you experience this orientation?

2. In which situations do you tend to act on this orientation?

3. Which influences and experiences have shaped your preference?

4. How are the learning objectives relevant to you?

Section 3
Building Cultural Skills

Building Cultural Skills

In section 1, we framed the notion of cultural competence and identified how the cultural orientations approach supports its development. In section 2, we assisted you in the interpretation and exploration of your own preferences toward key aspects of culture. This exploration will hopefully have (a) cemented the requisite open attitude, as well as self- and other-awareness, and (b) provided an anchor for gathering and organizing specific cultural knowledge.

In this section, we focus on the critical skill-set through which cultural competence is manifested. Previously identified and defined, cultural due-diligence, style-switching, and cultural mentoring, they have a significant role in a variety of domains for personal and organizational effectiveness.

The **Application Matrix** highlights this relationship and can guide you in identifying a learning and development strategy that matches your particular set of challenges. The exercises and worksheets that follow provide a process and tools for honing and exercising each of the critical skills.

Area of Application \ Cultural Skill	Cultural Due Diligence	Style Switching	Cultural Dialogue	Cultural Mentoring
1. Global Diversity Awareness and Inclusion Skills	Develop a broad knowledge of cultural patterns and their role in building and maintaining unproductive boundaries and barriers. Fine tune your observation and listening skills for the cultural content of interactions.	Develop a flexible behavioral repertoire along your strong/very strong orientations which allows you to maintain your sense of integrity and authenticity.	Develop the ability to bring about non-threatening, productive dialogue that enables shared responsibility for practices and processes meeting the needs of stakeholders.	Develop the ability to coach colleagues, partners, peers, and counterparts in the development and enhancement of adaptive skill needed in a new and differing cultural environment.
2. Leadership Development	Develop a general understanding of: (a) cultural underpinnings of specific business processes and management practices, and (b) the cultural success factors to business change initiatives.	Develop a flexible behavioral repertoire focused specifically on the environment, action, communication, and power dimensions (i.e, dimensions most directly related to people and relationship management).	Develop the ability to bring about non-threatening, productive dialogue enabling: (a) open discussion of cultural variation impacting performance, and (b) promotion of integration of practices.	Develop the ability to coach colleagues, partners, and reports in the development and enhancement of adaptive skills, to bridge cultural gaps, retain and/or motivate them, and foster personal development and growth.

Cultural Skill / Area of Application	Cultural Due Diligence	Style Switching	Cultural Dialogue	Cultural Mentoring
3. Global Business Assignments (incl. travel and relocation)	Develop a specific understanding of the critical cultural gaps affecting the effectiveness of a given international assignment as well as the cross-cultural adjustment process.	Develop targeted strategies for bridging specific cultural gaps.	Develop the ability to discuss the experiences of cultural gaps and adjustment in a manner conducive to effective conflict resolution and easing of tensions.	Develop the ability to facilitate your colleagues', partners', and reports' understanding of cultural gaps and bridging strategies to enhance their success.
4. Global Team Effectiveness and Inclusion	Develop a specific understanding of the critical cultural gaps affecting the effectiveness of the team and its members.	Develop a flexible behavioral repertoire focused specifically on the dimensions most directly related to teamwork and collaboration.	Develop the ability to discuss the cultural gaps affecting the team and actively promote the creation of an integrated "global team culture."	Develop the ability to facilitate cultural competence of your team members'.

Practice Guide to *Cultural Due Diligence*

Cultural Due Diligence is *the practice of assessing and preparing for the possible impact of culture.*

Given your particular business and management challenges, you may need to apply this skill broadly or very specifically.

Generally, this practice involves:

(1) determining the cultural backgrounds and orientations of one's colleagues, counterparts, partners, clients, and so on.

(2) evaluating potential and actual gaps, and

(3) developing a strategy for minimizing any resulting negative effects.

To facilitate this process for the national/societal level of culture, we have provided cultural orientations profiles for selected countries in Appendix A. The *Gap Analysis Worksheet* on the following page introduces a way for you to compare profiles and identify gaps.

Cultural due diligence on all levels of culture (national/societal, organizational, functional, and team) rests significantly on one's ability to analyze and interpret interaction patterns. To aid in building this skill, we have provided a guide for situation and interaction analysis.

To practice some of the basic elements of cultural due diligence, we have provided several critical incidents for you to analyze and interpret on page 110.

In Appendix D, please find additional references to resources that facilitate the practice of cultural due diligence.

Identifying Cultural Gaps

The information presented to you in the Regional COI Profiles in Appendix A is comprised of generalizations of dominant norms in a specific national/
societal environment. These profiles and the Gap Analysis Worksheet enable you to conduct a gap analysis and isolate the major challenges you *may* encounter when conducting business in these countries or interacting with individuals from these regions.

We recommend that you apply the following process.

On the Gap Analysis Worksheet, circle the cultural orientations indicated by your COI.

- Use Appendix A to identify the cultural orientations that tend to be very strong in the cultures of the countries in which you are interested, and mark them in the appropriate columns on the worksheet.

- Highlight those cultural dimensions in which your orientations differ from those of the national culture chosen, and mark them in the appropriate column.

- With the help of the information in Section 2, map out the main learning challenges you may encounter, and identify possible learning tools and strategies.

Gap Analysis Worksheet

	Your Preference	Country/ Region A	Country/ Region B	Country/ Region C	Gap	Strategies and Tactics
Environment						
Control	☐	☐	☐	☐		
Harmony	☐	☐	☐	☐	☐	
Constraint	☐	☐	☐	☐		
Time						
Single-Focus	☐	☐	☐	☐	☐	
Multi-Focus	☐	☐	☐	☐		
Fixed	☐	☐	☐	☐	☐	
Fluid	☐	☐	☐	☐		
Past	☐	☐	☐	☐	☐	
Present	☐	☐	☐	☐		
Future	☐	☐	☐	☐		
Action						
Being	☐	☐	☐	☐	☐	
Doing	☐	☐	☐	☐		

	Your Preference	Country/ Region A	Country/ Region B	Country/ Region C	Gap	Strategies and Tactics
Communication						
High Context	❑	❑	❑	❑	❑	
Low Context	❑	❑	❑	❑		
Direct	❑	❑	❑	❑	❑	
Indirect	❑	❑	❑	❑		
Expressive	❑	❑	❑	❑	❑	
Instrumental	❑	❑	❑	❑		
Formal	❑	❑	❑	❑	❑	
Informal	❑	❑	❑	❑		
Space						
Private	❑	❑	❑	❑	❑	
Public	❑	❑	❑	❑		
Power						
Hierarchy	❑	❑	❑	❑	❑	
Equality	❑	❑	❑	❑		

	Your Preference	Country/ Region A	Country/ Region B	Country/ Region C	Gap	Strategies and Tactics
Individualism						
Individualistic	❏	❏	❏	❏	❏	
Collectivistic	❏	❏	❏	❏		
Universalistic	❏	❏	❏	❏	❏	
Particularistic	❏	❏	❏	❏		
Competitiveness						
Competitive	❏	❏	❏	❏	❏	
Cooperative	❏	❏	❏	❏		
Structure						
Order	❏	❏	❏	❏	❏	
Flexibility	❏	❏	❏	❏		
Thinking						
Deductive	❏	❏	❏	❏	❏	
Inductive	❏	❏	❏	❏		
Linear	❏	❏	❏	❏	❏	
Systemic	❏	❏	❏	❏		

Situation and Interaction Analysis

The COI and the COM are excellent tools for cross-cultural situation-and interaction-analysis. The management of interactions and strategic action planning, as well as continuous learning and skill building can be accomplished by making the seven-step process described below part of your preparation and problem-solving process when encountering cross-cultural situations.

The worksheet on the next two pages provides a reproducible aid to facilitate your engagement in this process.

Step 1

Describe a situation/interaction to which you want to apply the analysis. This description needs to be detail focused on what you can observe in a nonjudgmental language.

Step 2

Identify the culture gaps that you have experienced or may experience as social distance. Ask yourself how the contextual components influenced/will influence those experiences and how they are manifested in your behavior and the behavior of those around you.

Step 3

Hypothesize how the other has experienced or may interpret the situation's contextual components.

Step 4

Explore various scenarios for coping with or adapting on all three levels (i.e., behavioral, cognitive, emotional), given each party's interests and understanding of context and goals.

Step 5

Select exercises to use in developing the identified coping skill or adaptation.

Step 6

Apply the practiced skill in the next interaction.

Step 7

Analyze results and revisit steps one through seven if necessary.

The Seven-Step Exploration Process of Interaction Analysis

Step 1
Describe the situation.

Step 2
Identify the culture gaps from your perspective (behaviorally).

Step 3
Hypothesize the other's experience (emotionally, cognitively and behaviorally.)

The Seven-Step Exploration Process of Interaction Analysis, page 2

Step 4
Explore and outline adaptations on these three levels.

Step 5
Identify the culture gaps from your perspective (behaviorally).

Step 6
Apply hypothesized adaptations.

Step 7
Analyze results.

Cultural Orientations at Work

The following exercises will help you sharpen your understanding of cultural orientations and the ways in which they can affect interactions in the workplace.

In the following six scenarios, each one presented illustrates a conflict based on diverging cultural orientations in business situations based on national/societal differences.

For each scenario:

- analyze the underlying culture gap (refer to Appendix A if necessary).

- identify possible strategies that would lead to a more desirable outcome.

- note your analysis in the space provided. Try to identify the link between behavior and cultural orientation.

When finished, you may refer to Appendix B for a brief discussion of each scenario.

Scenario 1

Mrs. Tamatsukuri, a Japanese employee of a U.S. company in Tokyo, is experiencing a problem. Frequently, Mr. Snyder, her boss and an expatriate from the United States, gives her what she sees as unrealistic timelines for completing her projects.

She manages to complete her work on time, but only through great personal sacrifice, such as working late, coming into the office on weekends, and getting her colleagues to assist her. Her boss is very pleased. He often praises her in weekly staff meetings and asks for her opinion in front of others.

When after several months Mrs. Tamatsukuri submits her resignation, citing family obligations as the official reason for leaving, Mr. Snyder is completely taken by surprise. Mrs. Tamatsukuri has, in reality, decided to seek employment with another company because of her guilt and shame for having been singled out by Mr. Snyder in front of peers. She also hopes she will be able to meet the demands of her new job without having to do so at such a high personal cost.

Your analysis:

Scenario 2

A major U.S. telecommunications company was working on a joint venture project with a Mexican communications company. On the first visit, Mr. Maddox, a senior engineer, headed the U.S. team. On the second visit, one of his subordinates led the team. Over the course of the next few scheduled visits, the composition of the U.S. team kept changing.

The Mexican team could not understand why different individuals would show up each time. The project was soon riddled with problems. The members of the Mexican team were reluctant to act on decisions and enact processes that had already been agreed upon because they did not feel they knew any of their U.S. counterparts well enough to trust them.

As a result, the Mexican team began to doubt the U.S. team's interest in both the project and the success of the relationship. When a competing telecom approached the Mexican company with a similar project, the Mexican company severed its relationship with its original U.S. partner who consequently lost significant market share in Latin America to its European rival.

Your analysis:

Scenario 3

Mr. Zheng, a Chinese manager with a lot of experience, knowledge and connections to key government, municipal, and business officials, has good rapport with Mr. Johnson, his contact from the U.K. parent organization that is engaged in a joint venture in China. When Mr. Johnson asked Mr. Zheng to postpone the meeting by months, Mr. Zheng replied, "I don't think it's a good idea. It would be better to go ahead with the meeting." Mr. Johnson started probing for reasons, but Mr. Zheng appeared unwilling to share information. The more Mr. Johnson probed the more defensive, closed, and vague Mr. Zheng's responses became.

On Mr. Johnson's insistence, the meeting was postponed. When the meeting finally took place, Mr. Johnson was upset that, against the previous commitment, the Chinese company sent only lower-level representatives unprepared to move the project along.

Your analysis:

Scenario 4

Mr. van Groet, a Dutch supervisor, is meeting with Mr. Al-Kathani, a Saudi Arabian, to provide feedback on his performance at work. "As you know, you're strong in most areas. There are a couple of areas where you could improve. One is in writing, which isn't easy for you, is it?" Mr. Al-Kathani looks down and simply says, "I see." Mr. van Groet continues, "Otherwise, there are no serious problems and, in general, you are doing a fine job." Mr. Al-Kathani, his glance still lowered, responds: "I'm very sorry to disappoint you, sir."

Your analysis:

Scenario 5

At the conclusion of an intensive English-language training program for a small group of Argentine managers who were preparing for assignments in the U.K., a graduation party was scheduled, and senior U.K. and Argentine company managers, the trainees, and their colleagues and families were invited. The trainees were asked to select a representative to give a speech in English at that event. Counter to the U.K. trainers' expectations, the group chose the most senior trainee, even though his English was the worst in the group. It was evident to each member in the Argentine group that only the highest-ranking individual could give such a speech.

Your analysis:

Scenario 6

On the first day of her new job, Erika, a Swedish woman, sat across from her new boss, Ms. Tanaka, and was somewhat perplexed at the issues her boss was emphasizing. Ms. Tanaka, a Japanese woman, pulled out a complicated flowchart that outlined the responsibilities of everyone in the office and how each activity affected others. She asked that Erika study the chart and spend her first day talking to her new coworkers so that she would become familiar with their activities and how they would affect her work and vice versa. At the end of the first day, Erika was visibly overwhelmed, particularly since she had expected to receive very clear instructions on the particular details of her job, not those of others.

Your analysis:

Practice Guide to *Style Switching*

Style-switching, i.e., *the ability to use a broad and flexible behavioral repertoire in order to accomplish one's goals,* is perhaps the most difficult and personal skill to develop. The central notion is that one has to act not on the basis of one's own preferences but on the basis of a counterpart's preferences and/or the requirements of a given situation in order to achieve personal or business goals.

It is critical to note this is a skill that is most required when one is emotionally least open or ready for it, namely when there is significant tension and pressure.

It entails an often prolonged, multistep learning process involving close scrutiny of one's behaviors, values, beliefs and emotions.

Success with style-switching involves:

- challenging and transcending the comfort zones of one's preferences and habits.

- experimenting with new ways of behaving.

- developing a mindset that approaches personal change openly and as an opportunity for enrichment rather than as a threat to personal integrity.

You may need to develop broad style-switching capabilities in preparation for the requirements of a multicultural environment or a specific capability to meet the challenges in a particular cultural environment. The following are designed to assist you.

- A series of style-switching scenarios that prompt you to suggest how individuals may need to change their behavioral approach. As identifying alternative behavioral approaches requires reflection and creative problem solving, these scenarios provide you opportunities for practice.

- Having practiced this type of reflection and creative problem solving with these scenarios, you may want to apply this perspective to some of your own challenges. To this end, we have provided a Worksheet that guides you to identify style-switching requirements associated with your strong and very strong cultural preferences.

- As style-switching requires a deep and personal engagement, we have provided some additional notes on this skill which we encourage you to review.

Style Switching Scenarios

In this part, you are presented with a series of scenarios requiring style-switching. For each, identify:

- (a) how the individual would approach the situation based on his/her cultural orientations and what would be the likely outcome?
- (b) how he/she could adapt his/her style to improve the outcome?

Scenario 1

A subordinate of Frank Huber's does not approach her job responsibilities with the thoroughness, attention to detail, and self-motivated, "empowered" manner that is expected of her. He has to let her know that this is causing great problems for the entire department and that she needs to change her behavior in order to keep her job. He is an indirect communicator who is equality-and harmony-oriented. His subordinate is a direct communicator who has a strong hierarchy and constraint orientation.

How would Frank Huber approach the situation based on his cultural orientations?

What would be the likely outcome?

How could Frank Huber style-switch?

How would this change the outcome?

Scenario 2

As a sales representative for AlphaCorp, Wendy Bokovski is making a presentation to a group of potential new clients. Her goal is to persuade them to purchase the new line of equipment the company released five weeks earlier. The decision makers in the group are deductive thinkers and expressive communicators with a past orientation to time. Her personal preferences are inductive, instrumental and future-oriented.

How would Wendy Bokovski approach the situation based on her cultural orientations?

What would be the likely outcome?

How could Wendy Bokovski style-switch?

How would this change the outcome?

Scenario 3

The motivation and morale of Mr. Ahn's team are low and the team members need to be energized in order to meet objectives. The situation is serious. Mr. Ahn is preparing to address his team at a social event that he has organized. Most of the team members are instrumental, informal communicators, future-oriented, and linear thinkers; they value equality and are universalists. This pattern of cultural orientations clashes with that of Mr. Ahn. He is an expressive communicator, present-oriented, a systemic thinker, a particularism, and he values hierarchy and formality.

How would Mr. Ahn approach the situation based on his cultural orientations?

What would be the likely outcome?

How could Mr. Ahn style-switch?

How would this change the outcome?

Scenario 4

Two colleagues of yours have been having a continuous personality conflict for several months now. Mr. Montello is an expressive, direct, and informal communicator with a strong public and particularistic orientation. He vents his anger and frustration openly. Ms. Heinz is an instrumental, indirect, private-oriented communicator who has a strong universalistic orientation. You have been asked to advise each on ways to resolve the conflict.

How would you advise Mr. Montello to approach Ms. Heinz?

What would be the likely outcome?

How would you suggest Ms. Heinz approach Mr. Montello?

How would this change the outcome?

COI Worksheet: Identifying the Value of Style Switching

To identify the value of style-switching may be useful in analyzing your own experiences and specific challenges associated with your cultural preferences. To this end we suggest to engage in the following exploration.

Step 1

Select one of your strong or very strong orientations. This should be an orientation that, based on your self-validation of your COI® profile, identifies a clear preference.

Step 2

Identify the specific situations and circumstances in which your behavior is guided by this preference (for example, when leading a meeting, when working under time pressure, when doing a performance review, when giving negative feedback, and so on).

Step 3

Identify the potential impact when you interact on the basis of this preference with someone who exhibits the opposite orientation or in a situation in which the opposite orientation is expected, rewarded and reinforced.

Step 4

Describe both the positive and the negative consequences that are associated with acting on your cultural preference.

Step 5

Explore how some of your specific performance challenges may be related to the dynamic you described in steps 3 and 4.

Step 6

Identify how style-switching could assist you to be more effective.

Considerations for Style Switching

It would be an utter mistake to assume that building adaptive behaviors and skills is equally possible and obtainable along all of the cultural continua of the COM. We have generally found that individuals have some preferences that are harder to change than others.

Consequently, some areas will present formidable challenges that you will not be able to overcome because the cultural orientation in question is so integral to your identity that changing it would result in a sense of compromising it.

Keep in mind that building your style-switching capabilities should enhance your effectiveness in realizing your goals, communicating your ideas, and successfully collaborating with others.

It is critical that you approach cross-cultural interactions with a clear sense of who you are and what the range of your flexibility is. It may help to think of some of your cultural orientations as non-negotiable or core identifying features and others as negotiable.

The **core** orientations identify preferences and behaviors that are intricately tied to your sense of self. They are essentially non-negotiable. You can build an awareness of the potential negative and positive aspects of these preferences and behaviors, but you will not feel comfortable altering them significantly.

The **negotiable** orientations consist of those preferences and behaviors in which you allow a range of flexibility and situational variability. This range of flexibility does not threaten your sense of self. The greater the number of behaviors you ascribe to the negotiable realm, the greater your ability to engage in style-switching.

It is important to recognize that the core and negotiable realms manifest themselves behaviorally and that they are therefore different from values. Because each cultural environment associates different behaviors with a similar value, building an extensive and flexible behavioral repertoire allows you to extend the very essence of your self. In fact, *the negotiable realm is the buffer through which your intentions, needs, requests and decisions can be translated across cultures.*

Following are two examples of people confronted with a situation in which either their core or negotiable cultural orientations were involved.

Martin Schutten

Martin Schutten, a native of Denmark, had worked at the local office for two years when he was promoted to product manager. With this promotion, he was expatriated to Venezuela to work at the Latin America branch. His role would be to oversee a team of engineers.

Unfamiliar with this plant and new to Venezuela, Martin had hoped that the team he was overseeing would provide him with a little guidance in regulations and procedures, etc. While he was very familiar with the product and expected that things would be carried out in a certain fashion, he also liked giving his employees the liberty to make certain decisions on their own, without always coming to him. This had worked quite nicely for him in his home office.

His new team of engineers, however, was not what he expected. They were always asking him questions that he felt could be answered without him. They made no decisions on their own. When Martin asked them about ways to change certain things, they did not provide suggestions. He was astounded that this team of educated workers could not give him any ideas or feedback.

His team members, on the other hand, were disconcerted by the lack of guidance from their new manager. They couldn't believe that their boss asked for their opinion or let them make certain decisions among themselves. They found that he was lacking in direction and confidence and they, in turn, felt that they could not function well without the guidance of a strong boss.

After a few weeks of ongoing confusion and frustration on both parts, Martin decided to seek the counsel of someone else. He contacted a colleague in Denmark who had lived and worked in Venezuela for six months but was not affiliated with this present team of engineers. His colleague was eager to share information as he had also had great difficulty integrating into his Venezuelan team. He found that Venezuelans greatly valued a hierarchical orientation. They did what was asked of them without asking questions, never skipped hierarchical lines, did not enjoy and were uncomfortable with brainstorming, and expected their team leader to have all of the answers. Martin's colleague also had a difficult time with these behaviors.

But as time went by and he learned to style-switch, his rapport with his team greatly improved and productivity increased.

Martin also enlisted the help of an informant within the organization who understood the organization and its culture. He asked his informant to provide tips and insights into directive behaviors that would make him more credible and successful with his team. In addition, Martin talked with other expats in the organization for any feedback and suggestions. After processing all of this information, Martin realized why his team didn't brainstorm or make their own decisions, and why they looked to him for so much guidance. The behaviors he had been expecting were NOT what their culture expected, reinforced and valued. The engineers were used to being told what to do and were not used to contradicting or offering suggestions to a superior.

While he couldn't imagine having to give orders to his team and to answer all questions without being questioned in return, he desperately wanted to find a solution. Every day, he observed his team, and slowly became a strong presence in their work area. He reinforced guidelines on a regular basis. He even practiced style-switching at home! He gave more direction to his cleaning people and asked his cooking staff to prepare something specific as opposed to letting them make their own cuisine decisions. In addition, through verbal and nonverbal communication, he let his domestic help know that he was the only one to make final decisions.

While Martin identified with the equality orientation to power and had grown up in a milieu where this was always emphasized and reinforced, he felt that his success as a team leader in Venezuela depended on his ability to style-switch. Although it was difficult, he was very committed to making this change. His will to learn about Venezuelan culture and to find ways to style-switch attributed to the success he had with his team. A short while after Martin started style-switching, he increased the trust of his team and was able to establish credibility and rapport with the team members.

Diana Cruz

For six years, Diana Cruz worked for the same company. One of her main reasons for choosing this company was its particularistic orientation. She could determine her work schedule, set up meetings when she thought it necessary, wear casual clothing and decide, on an individual basis, the specific needs of her clients.

Shortly after she had received a promotion, her company was acquired by another. Her company was downsized, and most of her colleagues were laid off. She, however, had been greatly valued within the original company and was not laid off.

Soon after the acquisition, she started having difficulties with the new management and company regulations. This company was very universalistic and had rigid policies and procedures. Diana had always valued a flexible work schedule to accommodate her busy personal life and odd working hours. With the new company, she had to comply with a set schedule. She felt that this was upsetting not only her outside needs, but also her creativity within the company.

In addition, when Diana wanted to schedule a meeting at her previous company, she would individually contact each person attending via an informal phone call, in person or through e-mail. If she wanted to schedule a meeting at the new company, she needed to send a formal e-mail to all of the attendees at least one week prior and to provide the meeting agenda.

While Diana enjoyed her work, she had also enjoyed the freedom, flexibility and consideration of her personal needs that her previous company had provided. She realized that, in order to continue with this company, she would need to comply with a long list of rules, regulations and policies.

Practice Guide to *Cultural Dialogue*

Cultural Dialogue is *the ability to elicit cultural insight through conversation, and thereby illuminate cultural underpinnings of behavior and performance, close cultural gaps and create cultural synergy.*

Based on our goals, we can distinguish two types of cultural dialogue:

1. Conversations with the primary purpose of raising awareness and knowledge about cultural differences. This type of conversation is a proactive measure for creating an inclusive environment and an understanding of differences.

2. Conversations with the primary purpose of identifying the cultural underpinnings of specific challenges that negatively affect collective performance. This type of conversation is a remedial measure for addressing the tensions, problems and issues related to cultural gaps.

Both types of conversations are powerful tools for establishing a new understanding and creating a shared foundation for thinking and acting. This ability to initiate and propel a *learning conversation* creates a new context for individual and collective action. It is a critical leadership skill in multicultural situations, such as mergers and acquisitions, global teams and so on.

The following provides:

■ Guide to Culture-based Challenges. This quick reference identifies the type of cultural issues that multicultural teams, groups, and/or organizations frequently face to the detriment of individual and collective performance.

■ Guidelines for Cultural Dialogue. This outlines an approach to help you to initiate and maintain learning conversations.

■ Cultural Dialogue Worksheet. This worksheet is designed to help you prepare for engaging in cultural dialogue and identifying the success of your learning conversations.

Guide to Culture-based Challenges

This quick reference identifies the types of challenges associated with cultural dimensions that multicultural teams, groups, and/or organizations frequently face to the detriment of individual and collective performance. The questions in the third column highlight some of the central questions that cultural dialogue can be used to address.

Cultural Dimension	Salient Organizational Challenges	Questions to Be Explored and Harmonized
Environment	■ Empowerment ■ Role Definition	Do individuals see and/or expect their individual role to be clearly limited and circumscribed? Do they see themselves empowered to take initiatives?
Time	■ Time Management ■ Problem Solution ■ Work-Flow Structure	How driven are individuals by timelines and deadlines? How are timelines and timeframes interpreted?
Action	■ Relationship Management ■ Planning ■ Decision Making	How much relationship building and/or team building is expected? What are the differing expectations for balancing relationship- and task-management? What are the expectations and needs concerning individual self-disclosure? How much discussion and reflection is customary before actions are taken (and/or decisions are made)?
Communication	■ Communication Media ■ Feedback and Conflict Management ■ Respect and Rapport	Which communication media do individuals prefer and how do they utilize them? How is utilization expected, rewarded and reinforced? In what ways do individuals expect feedback to be provided? What are the norms for each party involved?

Cultural Dimension	Salient Organizational Challenges	Questions to Be Explored and Harmonized
Communication (cont.)		How directly do individuals expect to address conflict? What is their comfort zone in addressing issues directly/indirectly? What kind of conflict management is expected, reinforced and rewarded? How much emotional alignment is expected in building rapport between parties?
Space	■ Information Sharing ■ Organizational Boundaries ■ Accountability	Do parties involved share information on a 'need to know' or a 'good to know' basis? To what degree do the parties involved accept shared accountability and authority? How much trust and relationship building is necessary for information to be shared?
Power	■ Authority ■ Decision Making ■ Hierarchical Relationships	How hierarchical are the decision-making processes within each individual group? What is expected, reinforced and rewarded? To what degree do individuals expect to operate with clear parameters of authority? What behaviors are associated with being a "manager" and a "report".
Individualism	■ Process, Rules and Identity ■ Reward and Recognition ■ Diversity	To what degree are the individuals involved motivated by group membership or as individual contributors? How are individuals rewarded and recognized for their contributions (a) as individuals and (b) as group/team members?

Cultural Dimension	Salient Organizational Challenges	Questions to Be Explored and Harmonized
Individualism (cont.)		To what degree are the parties involved attributed with *uniqueness* warranting special consideration and treatment?
		To what degree do parties and individuals involved expect to implement/follow a common set of rules and procedures?
Competitiveness	■ Work/Life Balance ■ Relationship to Work	To what degree do parties and individuals involved expect to separate work from family and social life?
		To what do the parties and individuals involved allow for a blending of these boundaries?
		What is expected, reinforced, and rewarded concerning the balance between work and among the parties involved?
Structure	■ Role and Process Clarity ■ Credibility and Trust	How clearly do processes and roles need to be articulated and framed?
		To what degree do parties involved expect clearly prescribed processes and defined expectations to invest them with credibility and trust?
		How is professional expertise associated with following and/or applying a given structure/process?
Thinking	■ Problem Solving ■ Presentation of Ideas	Do parties and individuals involved focus on the big picture or on specific details?
		Do parties and individuals involved expect experimentation or abstract reasoning to be used for problem solving?
		How do parties and individuals involved expect arguments and presentations to be structured? What is the preferred logical flow that is perceived as meaningful?

Guidelines for Cultural Dialogue

This outlines an approach to help you initiate and maintain learning conversations. Such a conversation can be divided into three distinct stages. For each stage, we provide a recommended approach as well as key factors for making this approach successful.

Stages	Recommended Approach	Success Factors
I. Initiation In this stage, you initiate the dialogue or learning conversation.	**Frame the conversation as a** Learning Alliance of the parties involved — rally behind a statement of purpose that acknowledges and invites different perspectives. **Articulate critical issues** — use the neutral, nonjudgmental vocabulary of the Cultural Orientations Model. **Extend an Invitation** — use non-threatening, constructive language to "invite" the parties involved to a joint exploration and problem-solving meeting.	Taking a facilitator's (third party's) perspective on the issue. Being conversant in the vocabulary provided by the Cultural Orientations Model.
II. Alignment and Shared Understanding In this stage, you create alignment between all parties involved as well as a shared understanding of the critical issues, interests and perspectives involved.	**Listen and Paraphrase** — pay attention to the articulated and unarticulated messages. Verify and clarify by articulating your interpretation and understanding. **Inquire and Probe** — ask non-leading, open-ended questions and lead counterpart to make general statements concrete and specific. **Share your perspective and/or experiences** — differentiate between behavior, intent/cultural drivers, and emotional impact. **Acknowledge** the perspectives involved-remember that acknowledgement does not mean agreement.	Having genuine curiosity in others' perspective, circumstances and viewpoints. Being open, authentic and persistent. Refraining from problem solving, and focus on understanding and clarifying. Clearly understanding the cultural underpinnings of your perspectives and experiences; in other words, distinct linkage between behaviors, intent, and emotional impact.

III. Joint Problem Solving	Identify Options	Being specific.
In this stage, you participate in shared problem solving to identify the possible ways in which to harmonize interests, bridge gaps and address resulting issues.	**Identify Options** — be creative in outlining possible solutions and approaches. Make sure that these options address the interests and needs of each party. **Jointly Visualize Success** — create and articulate both a general and a specific image of success. **Set Guiding Principles** – articulate principles that will guide actions and behaviors all parties recognize as constructive.	Talking through concrete examples.

Cultural Dialogue Worksheet

This worksheet follows a process to help you prepare for a cultural dialogue and identify the success of your learning conversations in instances where cultural differences pose significant challenges. Specifically, this worksheet will help you identify the statement of shared purpose, helping you initiate the conversation.

Guiding Questions	Notes
1. What do you observe? What are the behavioral patterns?	
2. What are your reactions to and interpretation of this pattern?	
3. What are the underlying cultural gaps (use the COM vocabulary)? What is *expected, reinforced, and rewarded* in given situations or contexts?	
4. What are the *undesired consequences* for you and the parties involved?	
5. How is your interest different from and/or compatible with the involved parties?	
6. How can you frame the purpose of the conversation by: (a) acknowledging the interests involved, and (b) expressing the desire to minimize the *undesired consequences?*	

Practice Guide to *Cultural Mentoring*

Cultural Mentoring is the ability to move an individual and/or group through cultural understanding to successful integration in a different cultural environment. While cultural dialogue is an important part of cultural mentoring, it also goes a step beyond as it is a sustained focus on assisting an individual or group to develop adaptive approaches in a new and different cultural environment.

This skill takes many different forms and may entail:

- assisting a new colleague in decoding the cultural norms of a new organization or team.

- coaching an international assignee manage the difficulties of culture shock.

- assisting a group calibrate its communication and work practices to increase effectiveness; e.g. within a differing dominant organizational culture or with a client organizational culture.

The steps identified in the *Cultural Mentoring Planning Guide* will assist you in enhancing this skill and applying it in your sphere of influence.

Cultural Mentoring Planning Guide

The following questions may guide you in identifying how you can apply cultural mentoring in your sphere of influence.

1. Who are the individuals or team/groups involved? _____
    _____
    _____

2. Which behavior patterns have you observed? (be specific about the situations and circumstances) _____
    _____
    _____

3. What are the underlying cultural gaps?_____
    _____
    _____

4. What are the unintended consequences of these gaps for the individual, group or organization involved? _____
    _____
    _____

5. What are specific behaviors that could close these gaps? _____
    _____
    _____

6. What is the likely outcome of not closing these gaps (i.e., not adapting the style or approach)? _____
    _____
    _____

7. What can be gained from adapting style or approach? _____
    _____
    _____
    _____

8. How can you assist the individual or group involved in developing adaptive insights and behaviors? What is your mentoring strategy? _____
    _____
    _____
    _____

Section 4

Putting It All Together

Cultural Skills in Action

This part is designed to help you to use cultural competence and the associated skills in a number of case scenarios. Each of the following scenarios exemplifies a particular type of cultural challenge.

Case 1: The Newcomer – encountering different work practices and expectations

Case 2: Relationship Management – managing a dilemma with a valued client

Case 3: Making a Presentation – selling effectively

Case 4: Negotiation Strategy – approaching negotiations

Case 5: Managing Performance – managing an employee effectively

Case 6: Social Responsibility – influencing and persuading successfully

Case 7: Delegation – managing for growth and development on an expatriate assignment

Case 8: Managing Upward – providing feedback to a manager

Case 9: Kula World Goes Global – leading a global team

For each of the scenarios, identify:

1. the cultural gaps that exist and may need to be bridged,

2. how each of the people involved may need to apply cross-cultural skills, and

3. the likely benefits of applying the necessary cross-cultural skills.

Case 1: *The Newcomer*

Kohei Wada, a fifty-year-old sales manager, recently joined a U.S. foreign capital electronics company in Japan. Much sought after, Wada joined only after much negotiation and with a lucrative contract in hand. During his first month on the job, he diligently studied all of the documents related to his job, performed official introductions with existing and potential customers and distributors, and began extensive rounds of socializing with his colleagues and subordinates.

Since Wada had come to the company highly recommended for his sales prowess, technical expertise, and English-language ability, Jonathan Collins, the U.S. president of the Japanese subsidiary, was somewhat disappointed by what he perceived as Wada's lack of initiative. So far, Wada had not presented a sales plan or offered an opinion during any of Collins' team meetings. Collins was especially nervous about the upcoming annual corporate sales meeting at the home office that both he and Wada were to attend. Collins was counting on Wada to give the U.S. Americans insights into the nature of the Japanese customer and the intricacies of dealing effectively with the Japanese distributors scheduled to handle a portion of their product line. As the meeting time drew near, Collins' disappointment did not abate. Nor did an opportunity to discuss the upcoming meeting in the United States present itself.

Busy until just minutes before the meeting, Collins barely had a chance to ask Wada about his flight from Japan, let alone brief him on his participation in the sales conference. At the meeting, the discussion almost immediately turned to a serious problem the Japanese subsidiary was having with its main distributor. The international sales manager, Chet Harper, directed his inquiry toward Wada: "Well, Kohei, any recommendations? You know Japanese distributors better than any one in this room."

Wada looked at Collins and said: "I think Collins-san has much more important experience. He knows best. I am just a newcomer."

Collins flinched and said: "Go ahead, Kohei, let everyone know what you think."

"Yes, Kohei," Harper said, "We'd really like to hear your opinion. It is crucial that we come up with a plan to solve this problem as soon as possible. We're counting on you to lead the way."

Wada stared at his hands, refusing to meet the eyes of anyone in the room. "I'm very sorry but I'm not prepared to give my recommendation. I am a newcomer and do not know enough to say anything." Annoyed and impatient, Harper focused on Collins: "Well, let's hear it, Jonathan. I don't have any more time to spend on this issue."

After presenting a possible solution to the problem, with no input from Wada, Collins was furious. When he caught up with Wada outside the conference room, he said: "Thanks a lot, Kohei. You'd better have a good explanation, because, right this minute, I'm not sure why the hell we hired you."

Case 2: *Relationship Management*

TCG, in line with its strategic direction to concentrate on its core business, has outsourced manufacturing of the PowerPac component to AREDON CORPORATION. This arrangement reduces production cost and increases speed as AREDON specializes in the manufacturing processes required. As profit margins for PowerPac have dropped significantly over the past two years due to fierce global competition, your company's competitive advantage is linked to both price and speed. AREDON's manufacturing capabilities in key low-cost international locations provides a good solution.

The TCG alliance manager is a **doing**-oriented, **direct** communicator with strong **universalist**, **cooperative**, and **deductive** orientations. You are **being** oriented, **indirect** communicator with strong **particularist**, **cooperative**, and **deductive** orientations.

You are the AREDON manager and have become frustrated with diminishing profit margins as your company has increased its demand for cost reduction. For AREDON, the PowerPac account is not a profitable undertaking and your boss has made it very clear that this trend cannot continue. You and the PowerPac manufacturer, however, value the relationship with TCG and have done everything in your power to adjust various processes, including waste management, to make up diminishing returns. The most recent request for cost reduction from TCG, however, is impossible to accommodate.

Case 3: *Making a Presentation*

As global product developers, you are making a presentation to a group of potential new clients. Your goal is to persuade them to purchase a new line of products the company is planning to launch next year. You have conducted a gap analysis and realize that the potential sources of social distance lie in the fact that the decision makers in the group are **deductive** thinkers and very **expressive** communicators. You know as well that they are **past-time** oriented.

Case 4: *Negotiation Strategy*

You are members of a team that is about to begin negotiations with an organization in another region. You want to ensure that negotiations go smoothly from the start. You have conducted a gap analysis and now realize that your counterparts are **being, fluid-time, flexibility** and **public space-**oriented.

This will potentially clash with your negotiating team's orientations along the **action, time, structure** and **space** dimensions, as your team is **doing, fixed-time, order** and **private space-**oriented.

Case 5: *Managing Performance*

Edgar Quinn employs an individual named Anna who is **competitive**, a **direct** communicator, and extremely **expressive** and **informal**. He himself is exactly the opposite: he is **cooperative**, an **indirect** and **instrumental** communicator and very **formal**. Unfortunately, Anna is not detail oriented. Nor does she follow instructions, even when things have been explained to her repeatedly. Mr. Quinn must find a way to approach Anna with guidelines and suggestions for paying closer attention to details and accomplishing her work more efficiently.

In the past, Mr. Quinn has attempted to give Anna constructive feedback on her performance in his customary way but it has yielded no results. He has now conducted a gap analysis and realizes that his own cultural orientations in the **competitiveness** and **communication** dimensions clash with Anna's.

Case 6: *Social Responsibility*

TCG in line with its strategic direction to concentrate on its core business, has out-sourced manufacturing of the PowerPac component to ARENDON CORPORATION. This arrangement reduces production cost and increases speed as AREDON is specialized in the manufacturing processes required.

As profit margins for PowerPac have dropped significantly over the past two years due to fierce global competition, your company's competitive advantage is linked to both price and speed. AREDON's manufacturing capabilities in key low-cost international locations provides a good solution.

Recently, ARENDON has received media attention for environmentally questionable waste management practices in two locations. Although local laws were not violated, the practices nevertheless are raising concerns among the environmentalist groups in North America and Europe. Because recent newspaper articles have implicated TCG, there is great concern about possible damage to the global image of the company. AREDON, on the other hand, has been a loyal and accommodating supplier whose competence and expertise have helped your company maintain a global leadership position with PowerPac.

Your are the TCG alliance manager. Your are a **doing**-oriented, **direct** communicator with strong **universalist**, **cooperative**, and **deductive** orientations. Your ARENDON counterpart is a **being** oriented, **indirect** communicator, with strong **particularist**, **cooperative**, and **deductive** orientations.

Case 7: *Delegation*

You are a recent expatriate responsible for managing customer support. After transferring in-country, you felt the reactions of some male managers to your role as a female manager first hand. You want to change that, but also want to be sensitive to local culture.

You have one female manager reporting to you. She is the least experienced manager you have. You want to make sure that she succeeds and have carefully selected assignments that offer her experience but little risk of failure. You're grooming her for a possible division assignment. You have talked to her formally and informally about her job and career. She's always positive and likes her work. However, you have a sense that she's not really happy. You think she might not be giving you direct feedback because she comes from a culture that emphasizes **harmony, constraint, cooperation,** and **hierarchy.**

You've also picked up some signs that male colleagues think you're being too easy with your female manager. You want to give her tougher assignments but don't want to jeopardize her chance to succeed. If she were to fail in any way, it could hurt other women and you for having given her "special treatment" What should you do?

Case 8: *Managing Upward*

You are the only female customer support manager in your country. You report to a female manager who is an expatriate. You expected that, being a woman, she would be supportive of your career. However, she has tended to give key assignments to your male colleagues and relegated you to less important accounts. This is hurting your career and reinforces some people's view of the work women should do. You have indicated your dissatisfaction to your manager in many ways, but she doesn't seem to understand.

Your manager is from a different culture, and you think that might be part of the problem. You compared your cultures.

Your Cultural Orientations	**Her Cultural Orientations**
Harmony and Constraint	Control
Being	Doing
High Context and Indirect	Low Context and Direct
Deductive	Inductive

Case 9: *Kula World Goes Global*

Having operated as a typical multinational organization for the past 70 years, Kula World is now committed to building an increasingly global organization. The rapid growth of global accounts has prompted the company to restructure operations in order to service global clients better and more cost-effectively, as well as leverage the advantages of global sourcing and manufacturing opportunities. Kula World has created global centers of excellence, operates as a matrix organization, and relies significantly on global, cross-functional teams.

For Karen Gilberts, a long-time employee from the U.K., all this translates into formidable challenges: She has been appointed leader of a core team of six. Their mission is to grow Kula World's most important global account, Japan's Nagadoshi Industries.

1. **Jackie O'Dell** from U.S. headquarters who has been supporting the client in the Americas region.

2. **John Kazuho**, a Japanese-American from Oakland, California, who was recently promoted to Key Account Executive for the client and who started his expatriate assignment in Tokyo only three months ago.

3. **Suguna Kumar,** from Bangalore, India, who heads a new team of software engineers in Bangalore who design applications for Kula World.

4. **Carlos Jimenez Castillo** from Juarez, Mexico, who manages the production plant in Juarez.

5. **Heinrich Schwartzkopf**, from Germany, who is the Director of Research and Development.

6. **Antonio Zanco**, Regional Marketing Director, originally from Italy, now in the midst of a two-year rotational assignment and based in Singapore.

Karen is concerned about the cultural issues that could emerge between people from such diverse backgrounds. She has had experience with cross-cultural teams in Europe and that was quite a struggle, but a team this diverse is new to her. Although she is familiar with some team members, she has not met everyone yet. In fact, it isn't really even a team yet, rather a group of individuals with varying roles and responsibilities. Creating a team is up to her.

Appendix A

Regional COI® Profiles

Country-Specific Cultural Orientations Profiles

In cross-cultural communication, perhaps in communication in general, it is advisable to assume difference until similarity is evident. The following charts provide cultural orientations profiles for a select number of national/societal cultures. They describe general norms and are therefore safer to assume than expecting cultural norms to be the same as your native cultural environment.

It is important to recognize that these charts are generalizations intended to provide comparison and contrast of major countries. They do not describe stereotypes, but rather offer assessments that can serve as initial hypotheses for understanding experiences in these national environments.

Generalizations differ from stereotypes in that:

-a generalization is a principle, statement, or idea having general, not specific, application. When applied to individuals, a generalization serves as a hypothesis to be tested and observed. It is based on an open attitude, insightful perception and an openness to learning.

-a stereotype is a belief about a person or group considered to typify or conform to one pattern, lacking any individuality. It is based on a judgmental attitude, a biased perception and a refusal to learn.

Therefore, when looking at the charts presented in this Appendix, remember that no

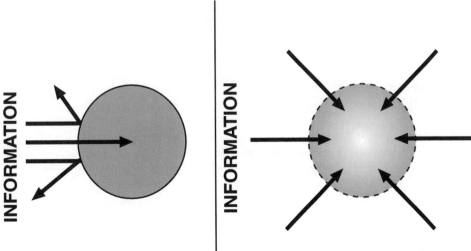

individual exactly corresponds to his or her national profile, within a country, significant cultural differences exist.

Cultural orientations generally have wide distribution among the residents of that country and the differences within one country can be and often are greater than the differences between countries.

We can refer to the bell-shaped curve below to understand the distribution of behaviors among people within a given population.

Most individuals in a particular culture may conform to a certain way of behaving or viewing the world. They therefore cluster along the top of the curve. Yet, a significant

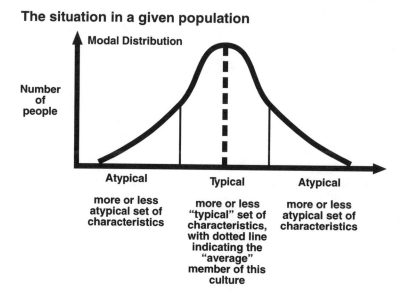

The situation in a given population

portion may differ from the norm and can be placed along their descending slopes of the curve. It is dangerous to use generalizations as predictive of individual behavior!

You should use this information to identify learning gaps and to guide you in selecting methods for developing your own adaptive skills, which can include, but are not limited to, training programs, specific readings, individual coaching, mentoring and self-directed learning programs.

AFRICA

REGIONAL COI ® PROFILES
Africa

COUNTRY \ DIMENSION	ANGOLA	NIGERIA	SOUTH AFRICA
1. ENVIRONMENT	Harmony/ Constraint	Harmony/ Constraint	Control/ Constraint
2. TIME	Multi-Focus Fluid Present	Multi-Focus Fluid Present	Multi-Focus Fixed/Fluid Past/Future
3. ACTION	Being	Being	Being/Doing
4. COMMUNICATION	High Context Indirect Expressive Formal	High Context Indirect Expressive Formal	High Context Direct Instrumental/ Expressive Formal
5. SPACE	Public	Public	Private/Public
6. POWER	Hierarchy	Hierarchy	Hierarchy
7. INDIVIDUALISM	Collectivistic Particularistic	Collectivistic Particularistic	Individualistic/ Collectivistic Particularistic
8. COMPETITIVENESS	Cooperative	Cooperative/ Competitive	Competitive
9. STRUCTURE	Order	Order	Flexibility
10. THINKING	Deductive Systemic	Deductive Systemic	Deductive/ Inductive Systemic

REGIONAL COI ® PROFILES
Asia

DIMENSION \ COUNTRY	AUSTRALIA	CHINA (PRC)	INDIA	JAPAN
1. ENVIRONMENT	Control/ Harmony	Control/ Harmony	Control/ Harmony/ Constraint	Harmony/ Constraint
2. TIME	Single-Focus Fixed Present/Future	Multi-Focus Fluid Present/Future	Multi-Focus Fluid Past/Present/ Future	Single-Focus Multi-Focus Fixed Past/Future
3. ACTION	Being/Doing	Being	Being	Being/Doing
4. COMMUNICATION	Low Context Direct Instrumental Informal	High Context Indirect Instrumental/ Expressive Formal	High Context Indirect Expressive Formal	High Context Indirect Instrumental Formal
5. SPACE	Private	Private/Public	Private/Public	Private/Public
6. POWER	Equality	Hierarchy	Hierarchy	Hierarchy
7. INDIVIDUALISM	Individualistic/ Universalistic	Collectivistic Particularistic	Collectivistic Particularistic	Collectivistic Particularistic
8. COMPETITIVENESS	Competitive	Cooperative/ Competitive	Cooperative/ Competitive	Cooperative/ Competitive
9. STRUCTURE	Flexibility	Order	Order/Flexibility	Order
10. THINKING	Inductive Linear	Inductive Systemic	Deductive Systemic	Inductive Systemic

REGIONAL COI ®PROFILES
Asia

COUNTRY / DIMENSION	KOREA	MALAYSIA	TAIWAN	THAILAND
1. ENVIRONMENT	Harmony/ Constraint	Harmony/ Constraint	Control/Harmony/ Constraint	Harmony/ Constraint
2. TIME	Multi-Focus Fluid Past/Future	Multi-Focus Fluid Present/Future	Multi-Focus Fluid Present/Future	Multi-Focus Fluid Past/Present
3. ACTION	Being/Doing	Being	Being	Being
4. COMMUNICATION	High Context Direct/Indirect Instrumental/ Expressive Formal	High Context Indirect Instrumental/ Expressive Formal	High Context Indirect Instrumental/ Expressive Formal	High Context Indirect Expressive Formal
5. SPACE	Public	Private/Public	Private/Public	Public
6. POWER	Hierarchy	Hierarchy	Hierarchy	Hierarchy
7. INDIVIDUALISM	Collectivistic Particularistic	Collectivistic Particularistic	Collectivistic Particularistic	Collectivistic Particularistic
8. COMPETITIVENESS	Cooperative	Cooperative/ Competitive	Cooperative/ Competitive	Cooperative
9. STRUCTURE	Order/Flexibility	Order/Flexibility	Order/Flexibility	Order
10. THINKING	Deductive Systemic	Inductive Systemic	Inductive Systemic	Deductive Systemic

EASTERN EUROPE

REGIONAL COI ®PROFILES
Eastern Europe

COUNTRY / DIMENSION	CZECH REPUBLIC	HUNGARY	POLAND	RUSSIA
1. ENVIRONMENT	Control/ Harmony/ Constraint	Control/ Constraint	Constraint	Constraint
2. TIME	Single-Focus/ Multi-Focus Fixed/Fluid Past/Future	Single-Focus Fixed Present/Future	Single-Focus Fixed Present/Future	Multi-Focus Fixed/Fluid Past/Present
3. ACTION	Being/Doing	Doing	Doing	Being
4. COMMUNICATION	High Context Indirect Instrumental/ Expressive Formal	High Context Direct Expressive Formal	Low Context Direct Expressive Formal	High Context Low Context Direct/Indirect Expressive Instrumental
5. SPACE	Public	Private/Public	Private/Public	Private/Public
6. POWER	Hierarchy/ Equality	Hierarchy	Hierarchy	Hierarchy/ Equality
7. INDIVIDUALISM	Collectivistic Particularistic	Individualistic/ Collectivistic Particularistic/ Universalistic	Individualistic Particularistic	Individualistic/ Collectivistic Particularistic
8. COMPETITIVENESS	Cooperative/ Competitive	Competitive	Competitive	Competitive/ Cooperative
9. STRUCTURE	Order/Flexibility	Order	Order	Order/Flexibility
10. THINKING	Inductive Linear/Systemic	Deductive Linear	Deductive Linear	Deductive Linear/Systemic

LATIN
AMERICA

REGIONAL COI ® PROFILES
Latin America

COUNTRY DIMENSION	ARGENTINA	BOLIVIA	BRAZIL	CHILE
1. ENVIRONMENT	Control/ Constraint	Constraint	Harmony/ Constraint	Control
2. TIME	Multi-Focus Fluid Past/Future	Multi-Focus Fluid Past/Future	Multi-Focus Fluid Present/Future	Multi-Focus Fluid Past/Future
3. ACTION	Being	Being/Doing	Being	Doing
4. COMMUNICATION	High Context Indirect Expressive Formal	High Context Indirect Expressive Formal	High Context Indirect Expressive Formal/Informal	High Context Direct Expressive Formal
5. SPACE	Public	Public	Public/Private	Private
6. POWER	Hierarchy	Hierarchy	Hierarchy	Hierarchy
7. INDIVIDUALISM	Individualistic/ Collectivistic Particularistic	Individualistic Collectivistic/ Particularistic	Individualistic/ Collectivistic Particularistic	Collectivistic Particularistic
8. COMPETITIVENESS	Cooperative	Cooperative	Cooperative/ Competitive	Competitive
9. STRUCTURE	Order/Flexibility	Order	Flexibility	Order
10. THINKING	Deductive Systemic	Inductive Linear	Deductive/ Inductive Systemic	Deductive Linear

LATIN AMERICA

REGIONAL COI ® PROFILES
Latin America

COUNTRY \ DIMENSION	COSTA RICA	EL SALVADOR	GUATEMALA
1. ENVIRONMENT	Harmony	Control	Control/ Constraint
2. TIME	Multi-Focus Fluid Past	Multi-Focus Fluid Past/Future	Multi-Focus Fluid Past
3. ACTION	Being	Being	Being
4. COMMUNICATION	High Context Indirect Expressive Formal	High Context Indirect Expressive Formal	High Context Indirect Expressive Formal
5. SPACE	Public	Public	Private
6. POWER	Hierarchy/ Equality	Hierarchy	Hierarchy
7. INDIVIDUALISM	Collectivistic Particularistic	Collectivistic/ Individualistic Particularistic	Individualistic Particularistic
8. COMPETITIVENESS	Cooperative	Competitive	Cooperative
9. STRUCTURE	Order/ Flexibility	Order	Order
10. THINKING	Inductive Systemic	Inductive Linear	Inductive Systemic

REGIONAL COI ® PROFILES
Latin America

COUNTRY DIMENSION	PERU	URUGUAY	VENEZUELA
1. ENVIRONMENT	Harmony/ Constraint	Control/ Constraint	Constraint
2. TIME	Multi-Focus Fluid Past/Future	Multi-Focus Fluid Past	Multi-Focus Fluid Present
3. ACTION	Being	Being	Being
4. COMMUNICATION	High Context Indirect Expressive Formal	High Context Indirect Expressive Formal	High Context Indirect Expressive Formal
5. SPACE	Public	Private	Public
6. POWER	Hierarchy	Hierarchy	Hierarchy
7. INDIVIDUALISM	Collectivistic Particularistic	Collectivistic/ Individualistic Universalistic/ Particularistic	Collectivistic Particularistic
8. COMPETITIVENESS	Cooperative	Cooperative	Cooperative/ Competitive
9. STRUCTURE	Flexibility	Order	Flexibility
10. THINKING	Inductive Systemic	Deductive Systemic	Deductive/ Inductive Systemic

REGIONAL COI ® PROFILES
North America

COUNTRY / DIMENSION	CANADA	MEXICO	U.S.
1. ENVIRONMENT	Control/ Harmony	Harmony/ Constraint	Control
2. TIME	Single-Focus Fixed Past/Future	Multi-Focus Fluid Future/Present	Single-Focus Fixed Present
3. ACTION	Being/Doing	Being	Doing
4. COMMUNICATION	Low Context Direct Instrumental Informal	High Context Indirect Expressive Formal	Low Context Direct Instrumental Informal
5. SPACE	Private	Public/Private	Private
6. POWER	Equality	Hierarchy	Equality
7. INDIVIDUALISM	Individualistic Universalistic	Collectivistic Particularistic	Individualistic Universalistic
8. COMPETITIVENESS	Competitive	Cooperative Competitive	Competitive
9. STRUCTURE	Flexibility	Order/Flexibility	Flexibility
10. THINKING	Deductive/ Inductive Linear	Deductive Systemic	Inductive Linear

REGIONAL COI ®PROFILES
Western Europe

COUNTRY DIMENSION	BELGIUM	FRANCE	GERMANY	ITALY	NETHERLANDS
1. ENVIRONMENT	Harmony Constraints	Control/ Harmony	Control/ Harmony	Constraint	Harmony
2. TIME	Single-Focus Multi-Focus Fixed Past/Present	Multi-Focus Fixed/Fluid Past/Future	Single-Focus Fixed Past/Future	Multi-Focus Fixed/Fluid Past/Present	Single-Focus Multi-Focus Fixed/Fluid Future
3. ACTION	Being/Doing	Being	Being/Doing	Being	Doing
4. COMMUNICATION	High Context Direct/Indirect Expressive Formal	High Context Direct/Indirect Instrumental/ Expressive Formal	Low Context Direct Instrumental Formal	High Context Indirect Expressive Formal	Low Context Direct Instrumental Formal/Informal
5. SPACE	Private	Private/Public	Private	Public	Private/Public
6. POWER	Hierarchy	Hierarchy	Hierarchy	Hierarchy	Equality
7. INDIVIDUALISM	Individualistic Universalistic Particularistic	Individualistic Particularistic	Individualistic Universalistic	Collectivistic Particularistic	Individualistic/ Collectivistic Universalistic Particularistic
8. COMPETITIVENESS	Cooperative/ Competitive	Competitive	Cooperative/ Competitive	Cooperative/ Competitive	Cooperative/ Competitive
9. STRUCTURE	Order/Flexibility	Order	Order	Flexibility	Order/Flexibility
10. THINKING	Deductive/ Inductive Linear	Deductive Systemic	Deductive Linear	Deductive/ Inductive Systemic	Deductive/ Inductive Linear

REGIONAL COI ® PROFILES
Western Europe

DIMENSION \ COUNTRY	NORWAY	SPAIN	SWEDEN	UNITED KINGDOM
1. ENVIRONMENT	Harmony	Control/ Constraint	Control/ Harmony	Control/ Constraint
2. TIME	Single-Focus Fixed Past/Future	Multi-Focus Fluid Past/Present	Single-Focus Fixed Past/Future	Single-Focus Fixed Past/Future
3. ACTION	Doing	Being	Doing	Being/Doing
4. COMMUNICATION	Low Context Indirect Instrumental Informal	High Context Direct/Indirect Expressive Formal	Low Context Direct/Indirect Formal Instrumental	Low Context Indirect Instrumental Formal/Informal
5. SPACE	Private	Private/Public	Private	Private
6. POWER	Equality	Hierarchy	Hierarchy	Hierarchy/ Equality
7. INDIVIDUALISM	Individualistic/ Collectivistic Universalistic	Individualistic/ Collectivistic Particularistic	Individualistic/ Collectivistic Universalistic	Individualistic/ Collectivistic Particularistic
8. COMPETITIVENESS	Cooperative	Cooperative/ Competitive	Cooperative/ Competitive	Cooperative/ Competitive
9. STRUCTURE	Order	Order/Flexibility	Order	Order
10. THINKING	Deductive Systemic	Deductive/ Inductive Systemic	Inductive Linear	Inductive Linear

Appendix B

Scenario Explanations

Possible Scenario Explanations

Scenario 1

Mrs. Tamatsukuri's harmony orientation as well as her indirect, hierarchy, and collectivistic orientations are clashing with Mr. Snyder's expectations. Although she has been trying hard to accommodate her boss, she has only managed to do so at the cost of suffering extreme personal stress and her feeling that she had compromised her colleagues, coworkers and friends (collectivistic orientation). She was also extremely uncomfortable being singled out for praise or for her opinion as she is a collectivist who views all accomplishments as group successes. As the pressure on her increased, she felt that she could not address the problem openly with Mr. Snyder (hierarchy and/or indirect orientation). She sees no other solution than to resign from her position.

Scenario 2

In this scenario, the teams are clashing along the action, individualism and structure dimensions. The U.S. team is a collection of individualists, each pursuing his or her own self-interest (individualistic orientation). Furthermore, the U.S. team members may not see the frequent changes in team composition as a major obstacle to getting the work done (doing orientation) and they may expect changes in team composition as a normal way of working (flexibility orientation). The Mexican team, on the other hand, requires stable and predictable relationships between trusted individuals before committing to the work at hand (being, order and collectivistic orientations).

Scenario 3

Mr. Zheng is an indirect and high-context communicator with a strong being orientation. He requires trusting relationships before business can be conducted (being orientation) and expects that, on the basis of this trust, communication is implicit and presumes shared frame of reference (high-context orientation). He was embarrassed and annoyed by Mr. Johnson's requests for more information and he interpreted the behavior as distrust. He assumed that Mr. Johnson would understand the importance and significance of the meeting. His indirect orientation did not allow him to address this conflict explicitly, so he expressed his feelings by becoming increasingly closed, vague and diffuse in his responses.

Scenario 4

Mr. van Groet's direct, low-context, and individualistic orientations are clashing with Mr. Al-Kathani's indirect and hierarchy orientations. Although Mr. van Groet intended his evaluation to be overwhelmingly positive, his direct style of communication was understood by Mr. Al-Kathani, as sharp criticism, and Mr. Al-Kathani feels deeply embarrassed (high-context orientation) and ashamed that he disappointed his superior. He can neither argue with his supervisor (hierarchy orientation) nor discuss the situation explicitly (high-context/indirect orientation).

Scenario 5

Based on their collectivistic orientation, the U.K. instructors expected their Argentine students to select the best speaker of English to represent the group. Although the Argentine managers share a collectivistic orientation with their U.K. teachers, they differ significantly from their U.K. colleagues in their hierarchy orientation. The hierarchy orientation of the Argentines is much stronger than that of the U.K. instructors. Consequently, it was of overriding concern to the Argentines to select the most senor member of their group to represent them, regardless of his English-speaking abilities. To do otherwise would have seemed extremely insubordinate and rude to them.

Scenario 6

Both parties to this interaction conflict on the structure and thinking dimensions of culture. Her request for and reference to a flowchart reveals Ms. Tanaka's systemic orientation to work. She expected Erika to develop a good understanding of the relationships between tasks and functions in order for Erika to understand her own job. Erika's consternation originated from her more linear orientation to thinking, which meant that she would have preferred to focus on individual tasks rather than taking a holistic view of her job. Secondly, Erika's order orientation to structure clashed with Ms. Tanaka's flexibility orientation. Erika expected a clear and detailed job description (order orientation) while Ms. Tanaka expected Erika to feel comfortable spending her day gathering information in a rather unstructured way (flexibility orientation).

Appendix C

Definition of Key Terms

Definition of Key Terms

Being: A cultural orientation that identifies a preference for relationship-centered behaviors and values.

Collectivistic: A cultural orientation that identifies a preference for subordinated individual interests to group interests. Identity is based on the social network, and behavior on social obligation.

Competitive: A cultural orientation that identifies a prefered emphasis on achievement and material success-oriented behaviors and values.

Control: A cultural orientation that identifies a prefered belief that people can and should dominate their environment and change circumstances to fit human needs.

Constraints: A cultural orientation that identifies a belief that people should accomodate their ciercumstances and conditions.

Cooperative: A cultural orientation that identifies values and behavior that emphazise quality of life and interdependence.

Cultural continuum: The spectrum between two opposing orientations within a cultural dimension.

Cultural competence: A key global leadership competency characterized by the ability to convert an awareness of cultural orientation patterns and one's own cultural profile into behaviors through which to connect and be successful with a culturally diverse workforce and customer base.

Cultural dialogue: The ability to illuminate cultural underpinnings of behavior and performance, close cultural gaps, and create cultural synergy through conversation.

Cultural dimension: An overall category that contains one or more related cultural continua.

Cultural mentoring: The ability to advise, teach, and coach the individuals in one's sphere of influence to (a) recognize the cultural underpinnings and consequences of their behavior, (b) understand the cultural and behavioral requirements for true inclusion, and (c) support change through inclusive behaviors, practices, and approaches (including policies and systems).

Cultural orientation: A particular cultural-based value that forms the underpinning of behaviors and expectations.

Cultural Orientations Indicator or COI: A personal assessment tool that provides individuals with their own cultural profile on the basis of the conceptual framework described by the Cultural Orientations Model (COM).

Cultural Orientations Model or COM: A model of culture introduced in 1995 that combines key concepts of intercultural studies into 10 cultural dimensions, 17 cultural continua and 36 cultural orientations.

Cultural preference: An overall favoring of a particular cultural orientation, perspective or approach.

Culture: The complex pattern of ideas, emotions, and observable manifestations (behaviors and/or symbols) that tend to be expected, reinforced, and rewarded by and within a particular group.

Culture gap: The difference in cultural orientations between individuals or between an individual and a social context.

Deductive: A cultural orientation that describes reasoning based on theory, concepts and abstract logic.

Direct: A cultural orientation that identifies a preference for explicit one- or two-way communication and conflict management.

Doing: A cultural orientation that identifies a preference for task-centered, productive activity and achievement of goals.

Equality: A cultural orientation that identifies a preference for the minimization of levels of power.

Expressive: A cultural orientation that identifies a preference for emotiotional an emotive and communication style.

Fixed: A cultural orientation that identifies a preference for precisely defined punctuality.

Flexibility: A cultural orientation that identifies a tolerance for unpredictable situations, ambiguity and uncertainty.

Fluid: A cultural orientation that identifies a preference for punctuality defined loosely.

Formal: A cultural orientation that identifies a preference for protocol and decorum.

Future: A cultural orientation that identifies a preference to trade short-term gain for long-term results.

Gap analysis: The act of contrasting and comparing cultural orientations between individuals or an individual and a social context in order to identify appropriate behavioral strategies for improved communication.

Harmony: A cultural orientation that identifies a preference for compromise and balancing needs.

Hierarchy: A cultural orientation that identifies a preference for power differences between individuals and/or among groups.

High context: A cultural orientation that identifies a prevalence of implicit communication, i.e. messages and expectations are communicated without needing to be stated explicitly.

Indirect: A cultural orientation that identifies a preference for implicit conflict management.

Individualistic: A cultural orientation that identifies a focus on individual independence and self-interest over group affiliation and obligation, as well as the value of individual independence and accountability.

Inductive: A cultural orientation that identifies a preference for reasoning based on experience, experimentation and cases.

Informal: A cultural orientation that identifies a preference for dispensing with ceremony and protocol.

Instrumental: A cultural orientation that identifies a preference for a dispassionate and impersonal communication style.

Interaction analysis: The analysis of interpersonal communication processes in order to gain a better understanding of each party's values, expectations and objectives.

Linear: A cultural orientation that identifies a preference for analytical thinking that breaks problems into discrete components.

Low context: A cultural orientation that identifies a prevalence for explicit communication, i.e. messages and expectations are communicated primarily through words.

Multi-focus: A cultural orientation that identifies a preference for engaging in multiple tasks and relationships simultaneously.

Order: A cultural orientation that identifies a prevalence of a high need for predictability and certainty.

Particularistic: A cultural orientation that identifies a prevalence of social network how focus is placed on obligations before abstract rules, often accompanied by a sense of uniqueness.

Present: A cultural orientation that identifies a preference for a short-term focus aimed at quick results.

Private: A cultural orientation that identifies a preference for clearly demonstrated boundaries, including physical distance.

Public: A cultural orientation that identifies a preference for loose boundaries and close proximity.

Single-focus: A cultural orientation that identifies a preference for focusing on one task at a time.

Situation analysis: The analysis of social contexts in order to gain a better understanding of the meaning, requirements and expectations embedded in social situations.

Social distance: The level of comfort or discomfort between individuals or groups as a result of differences in cultural orientations.

Style switching: The ability to effectively employ a broad and flexible range of behaviors to attain a desired outcome.

Systemic: A cultural orientation that identifies a preference for holistic thinking that is focused on the big picture and the interrelationships of components.

Universalistic: A cultural orientation that identifies a preference for abstract rules before social network obligations.

Appendix D
References and Additional Resources

References

Hall, Edward T. *Beyond Culture*. New York: Doubleday, 1981.

Hampden-Turner, Charles, and Alfons Trompenaars. *The Seven Cultures of Capitalism: Value Systems for Creating Wealth in the United States*, Japan, Germany, France, Britain, Sweden and the Netherlands. New York: Doubleday, 1993.

Hofstede, Geert. *Cultures and Organizations: Software of the Mind*. London: McGraw-Hill, 1991.

Hofstede, Geert. *Culture's Consequences: International Differences in Work-Related Values*. Beverly Hills, CA: Sage, 1980.

Isaacs, William. *Dialogue and the Art of Thinking Together*. New York, NY: Doubleday, 1999.

Kluckhohn, Florence R., and Strodtbeck Frederick L. *Variations in Value Orientations*. Westport, CT: Greenwood Press, 1961.

Kroeber, Alfred L., and Kluckhohn Clyde *Culture: Critical Review of Concepts and Definitions*. Vol. 1, No. 1. Cambridge, MA: Peabody Museum, 1952.

Rhinesmith, Stephen H. *A Manager's Guide to Globalization*. Homewood, IL: Irwin, 1993.

Rhinesmith, Stephen H. *Cultural Organizational Analysis: The Interrelationship of Value Orientations and Managerial Behavior:* Cambridge, MA: McBer and Company, 1971.

Rosen, Robert, Patricia Digh, Marshall Singer, and Carl Phillips. *Global Literacies*. New York, NY: Simon & Schuster, 2000.

Stewart, Edward C., and Milton J. Bennett. *American Cultural Patterns: A Cross-Cultural Perspective*. Yarmouth, ME: Intercultural Press, 1991.

Stone, Douglas, Bruce Patton, and Sheila Heen. *Difficult Conversations: How to Discuss What Matters Most*. New York, NY: Viking, 1999.

Training Management Corporation. *Doing Business in Regions and Countries Around the World Series*. Princeton, NJ: Princeton Training Press, 2000.
Trompenaars, Alfons. Riding *the Waves of Culture: Understanding Cultural Diversity in Business*. London: The Economist Books, 1993.

Viney, John. *The Culture Wars*. Oxford, UK: Capstone Publishing Limited, 1997.

Walker, Danielle, Thomas (Tim) Walker, and Joerg Schmitz. *Doing Business Internationally*. Second Edition. New York: McGraw-Hill, 2003.

Additional Resources

A suite of web tools and training solution publications, have been developed to support the cultural orientations approach to building cultural competence.

1. The Cultural Navigator™ - A TMC Web Tool

The Cultural Navigator is a management resource for cross-cultural business solutions. It is a gateway to eight adaptable learning channels:

❑ **myNavigator:** A personal navigation system based on:

User profile:
- Business traveler
- Expatriate/repatriate
- Manager with global reach
- Global/virtual team member or leader
- COM/COI practitioner

Individualized navigational *dashboard*:
- Pre-selected links that correspond to user profile
- Cultural Navigator™ database resources that are tailored to user needs

Print and e-mail version of a *personal development plan*
- Management tracking capability
- Ability to link to corporate training and development
- Enable an embedded needs analysis with reports

❑ myNavigator Channel: **Cultural Profile** - Take your Cultural Orientations Indicator (COI®), a validated cultural assessment tool for building cultural and global management competence.

❑ myNavigator Channel: **CountryScope** - Access a country database offering economic, cultural and management information as well as a COI profile for 100 countries.

❑ myNavigator Channel: **Learning Zone** - Participate in web-based, virtual and on-site Learning Labs designed to enhance and develop global management competencies.

❑ myNavigator Channel: **Global Management Toolbox** - Access InfoPacks™ that approach a wide array of cross-cultural issues with tools for the global manager.

❑ myNavigator Channel: **Research Zone** - Access current TMC research results, conduct individual research and participate in current research studies.

❑ myNavigator Channel: **Global Learning Exchange** - Engage in communities of users sharing a common interest, profile and/or learning objectives.

❑ myNavigator Channel: **The Bookstore** - one-stop access to books and media supporting global management effectiveness.

❑ myNavigator Channel: **Ask the Expert** - 24/7 access to experts and advisors in the field of cross-cultural management and global organization effectiveness.

Visit the Cultural Navigator at **www.culturalnavigator.com**

2. Doing Business in Countries and Regions

This series consists of 31 country-specific publications and 6 region-specific publications. The information provided is fully integrated with the Cultural Orientations Model and provides a comprehensive introduction to the social and business culture of the specific country and region.

The following publications are available in print or pdf versions:

COUNTRY

Argentina	**India**	**South Africa**
Australia	**Ireland**	**South Korea**
Belgium	**Italy**	**Spain**
Brazil	**Japan**	**Sweden**
Canada	**Malaysia**	**Switzerland**
Chile	**Mexico**	**Thailand**
China	**Netherlands**	**U.K.**
Colombia	**Norway**	**U.S.**
France	**Philippines**	**Venezuela**
Germany	**Saudi Arabia**	
Hong Kong	**Singapore**	

REGION

Asia
Eastern Europe
Latin America
Middle East and North Africa
North America
Western Europe

To order, contact Princeton Training Press at **609-951-9319** or go to:
www.tmcorp.com

3. Culture in Management

This series extends the cultural orientations approach to specific domains of management. Each publication embeds the treatment of the given topic with a thorough cross-cultural perspective and supports managers with global responsibilities.

The following titles are available in print or pdf versions:

- **Doing Business Internationally**
- **Influencing and Persuading Across Cultures**
- **Managing Across Cultures**
- **Managing Global Projects**
- **Transcendent Teams™**
- **Marketing and Sales Across Cultures**
- **Negotiating Across Cultures**
- **Presenting Across Cultures**

To order contact Princeton Training Press at **1-609-951-9319** or go to: **www.tmcorp.com**

4. Training Solutions

The following workshops and training solutions are recommended to support the application of the cultural orientations approach to the global workplace:

- **Cultural Orientations at Work**
- **Doing Business Globally**
- **Managing Across Cultures**
- **Managing Culture in Global Business**
- **Multicultural Teamwork**
- **Leading Global Teams**
- **Global Project Management**
- **Negotiating Across Cultures**
- **Presenting Across Cultures**

In addition, country- and region-specific overview workshops are available and can be customized to an organization's learning needs.

Visit TMC at **www.tmcorp.com** or call 1-609-951-0525.

DOING BUSINESS INTERNATIONALLY, Second Edition. New York: McGraw-Hill, 2003. Danielle Walker, Thomas (Tim) Walker, & Joerg Schmitz.

Description

Doing Business Internationally is today's single best resource for managing multicultural organizations in a global marketplace. This powerful book has helped thousands of executives understand divergent cultures and improve their leadership effectiveness across organizations, industries and borders.

Now, as the world continues to shrink and its opportunities expand, this completely revised and updated second edition builds upon the groundbreaking lessons from the original, while providing all-new navigational tools and techniques. Along with valuable case studies and examples of effective multicultural leadership skills, it features:

- The versatile and valuable Cultural Orientations Model™ (COM™)
- The Cultural Orientations Indicator®- a unique cross-cultural assessment tool based on the COM™
- In-depth analysis of the impact of culture at the individual, team/group, organizational and country/regional levels

Over the past decade, *Doing Business Internationally* has shown thousands of global executives how to move beyond borders to succeed in all cultural environments. Now, let this updated edition show you how to make yourself understood and- just as importantly- understand others in today's newly demanding, cross-cultural marketplace.

Target Audience

Anyone who wants to understand the impact of key global trends and cultural differences at the individual, team and organizational levels and wishes to adapt business skills and competencies for greater effectiveness in cross-cultural interactions.

Contents

Foundational Knowledge

- Chapter 1: The Global Environment
- Chapter 2: Culture
- Chapter 3: The Cultural Orientations Model™
- Chapter 4: A Survey of Cultural Patterns
- Chapter 5: Cultural Orientations in Communication
- Chapter 6: Cultural Competence in Marketing and Sales
- Chapter 7: Translating Global Vision Into Local Action: Focus on Multicultural Teamwork and Collaboration

About the Authors

Danielle Medina Walker is founder and president of Training Management Corporation. Fluent in four languages, Ms. Walker has worked and consulted extensively with major companies in North America, Asia, Europe, and the Middle East, and is coauthor of several books on achieving global professional success. She can be reached at dwalker@tmcorp.com.

Thomas Walker is chief operating officer of Training Management Corporation (TMC), a recognized leader in the field of global management and cross-cultural consulting and training. A veteran of over two decades in international human resources development, Mr. Walker spent a number of years living and working overseas. He can be reached at twalker@tmcorp.com.

Joerg Schmitz is director of Training Management Corporation. A cultural anthropologist by training, Mr. Schmitz specializes in consulting on strategic global leaning initiatives and delivering management training to global companies and organizations both in the United States and overseas. He can be reached at jschmitz@tmcorp.com